The Neuro-Com Program

How to Reprogram Your Mind,
Beat Anxiety and Depression,
and Create a New Future

An Exposé of How You Can Control
Your Thoughts, Emotions
and Destiny Using
the Neuro-Com Program

The Neuro-Com Program

How to Reprogram Your Mind, Beat Anxiety and Depression, and Create a New Future

GARY W. JOHNSTON

© 2000, 2013 Gary W. Johnston

All Rights Reserved.

No part of this publication may be reproduced, stored in a retrieval system, or transmitted, in any form or by any means, electronic, mechanical, photocopying, recording, or otherwise, without the written permission of the author.

Published by GMF International Pty. Ltd., Victoria, Australia
P.O. Box 16, Bulleen VIC 3105 Australia
Telephone +61 3 8682 8772
Email: gmf@gmfint.com
Website: www.gmfint.com
Neuro-Com support website: www.neuro-com.org

ISBN: 978-145752-389-2
This book is printed on acid-free paper.

Printed in the United States of America

Contents

A Study in Mind Communications 1

Functional NeuroDynamics 1
    The course structure 2
    How to use this program 4
    The Neuro-Com website 7

Chapter One Human Drives and Limiters 9

The Global Problem 9
    Success, mediocrity, and failure 10
    The powerful mechanism of "NOW" 13

The Six D's: The First Steps on the Path 15
    1. Decision 17
    2. Desire 19
    3. Direction 21
    4. Discipline 23
    5. Determination 25
    6. Daily method of operation 26

Chapter Two How Your Mind Really Works 29
    The Conscious Mind—Gateway to NOW 31
    Your Unconscious Mind: The Gateway to the Past 34
    Your Memory's Emotional Time Bomb 36
    Dr. Hamer's Research: A Summary 39
    The Critical First Five Years 41
    Beliefs, Values, Attitudes, and Behaviour 43
    Internal Conflicts 44
    Emotions and Behaviour 45
    Fast-track Life Enhancement 47
    Your "Soul" 48

Chapter Three Possible Blocks to Your Progress 51

Biochemical Blocks to Progress 51

Contents

    Typical symptoms of psycho-nutritional deficiency 57
    Nutritional suggestions for everyone 59
    Deadly foods 60

Changing our Environment 62
    Being susceptible to the negative influences of others 62
    The Principle of Edification 63
    The Principle of Vacuum 66

Chapter Four Communicating with Your Mind 73

Neuro-Com 73
    Sight, touch, smell, taste, and sound 74
    Your Personal Neuro-Com 79
    Your Strategies Exercise revisited 82
    Making friends with your unconscious mind 88
    Example awareness 90
    Taking Control 92

Chapter Five   Practical Neuro-Com 93

Stacking the Deck in Your Favour 93
    Conscious Observation 94
    Unconscious Observation 94
    Neutralising negative emotional responses 96

NeuroDynamic Detachment 98
    Removing Anxiety or Anger 98
    Dissolving guilt forever 101
    Self-image: Removing the conflict 104
    A History of self-image conflict and emotional trauma during early life 105
    Other Memory Conflicts 110

Your Values System 114
    Why are your values important? 115

Chapter Six Designing Your Future 121

Past—Present—Future 121
    The Design of Your Timeline 122
    Your NeuroPrint 124

Creating the Plan 127
    1. Creating Balance in your future 128
    2. Creating your 10-year plan 129

    The Rules of Designing Good Goals 130
    Writing Your Life Plan 131
    NeuroPrint Goals for My 10-Year Plan 134
    NeuroPrint Goals for My 5-Year Plan 135
    NeuroPrint Goals for My One-Year Plan 136
    NeuroPrint Goals for My Six-Month Plan 137

What do you need to value? 138

Chapter Seven Designing future memory 149

Balancing Values with Goals 149
    Important learning you should understand 150
    Making Goals Congruent with Your Values 150
    Evaluating your results 161
    What do I need to value? 162
    Values Needed to Create a Lifestyle Goal 165
    Values Needed to Create a Health Goal 166
    Values Needed to Create a Family Goal 167
    Values Needed to Create a Relationships Goal 168
    Values Needed to Create a Personal Development Goal 169
    Changing energy in values 175
    Your Master Neuro-Com Characteristics Checklist for Positive Outcomes
    and 177
    Removing undesirable behaviours 179

Chapter Eight Creating happiness 183

Balancing success with personal happiness 183
    What makes happiness a reality? 184
    What stops most people from being happy? 185
    The highest intent of your mind 187
    Neuro-Com in relationships—Doing it with others! 188
    "The problem with relationships is......". 189
    Expectations 191
    The first step to NOW 193
    Communication in relationships 195
    The Foundations of Humanity 195
    Why are relationships so important? 197
    The NeuroDynamics of Relationships 198
    The ideal relationship 201
    The Elusive SOUL Partnership 204

Establishing Your Relationship Values 206

Contents

Chapter Nine Where to from here? 219

Neuro-Com and Spiritual Evolution 219

The End and the Beginning..222

A Study in Mind Communications

FUNCTIONAL NEURODYNAMICS

We live in a dysfunctional world. Often, we accept our situation and do nothing to change our circumstances, believing we have no power to swim against the tide.

This course will give you a very different perspective and PROVE that **you** have control over your circumstances. **You** have the capacity to live the kind of life you want and develop the relationships, income, security, and lifestyle of your dreams.

Before we begin, please understand something very clearly. This book is not going to tell you to think positively, write affirmations, or sing songs of praise to the moon while standing on one foot and rubbing your head. The trendy self-improvement methods of the 1970s and 80s sounded wonderful. But very few people experienced significant results and virtually no one achieved permanent change. A lot of authors made a lot of money (so I guess their methods worked for them but for very different reasons).

This program is the result of 40 years of intense research, both theoretical and practical. Thousands of hours of clinical work across 35 years with individuals and groups have proven a very interesting theory about how your mind works, how it creates your behaviour, and hence how it forms your lifestyle and its limitations.

With millions of words written about hundreds of mind-change techniques, the way to create change in your life is to communicate with your unconscious programs. It is incredibly SIMPLE. By understanding the way your unconscious mind really works, and your conscious relationship with it, you can easily develop a powerful personal strategy that will command your unconscious mind to do exactly what you want.

You can change your reaction to your environment and emotions instantly.

This program is carefully graded over eight chapters so that the work you do will become second nature to you. It is important that you make the decision now to set aside some time to understand the program's basic tenets and then work through the exercises. I assume that because you bought this book, you are not completely happy with your existing life. If you are happy with your life as it is or you are not willing to take the time to follow through with this program, give this book to someone who will make use of it.

THE COURSE STRUCTURE

This course is based on both experience-based knowledge and theory combined with practical exercises that prove to your unconscious mind that YOU are in control. You will soon come to understand that creating change is a simple process. There is nothing mystical about it — just solid common sense and a clear understanding of "**Neuro-Com**."

You may have to relinquish some television time over the next several months as you progress through the program. There are many exercises to complete that require your concentration. They are not difficult, but much like learning to ride a bike, practice is essential to become proficient.

The first chapter identifies the source of limitations and restrictive behaviours your mind uses to create your environment. You will understand how and where these behaviours were created and how the different parts of your mind function to maintain behaviours that seem to be detrimental to you. You will understand clearly why you really are the controller and in control of your present and your future. Even your emotions, anxieties, fears, anger, and hate can be changed within seconds. In this first chapter, you will take your first steps toward the future you want.

The next three chapters look at some of the physical causes of limitations in thinking and what you can do to increase the clarity and focus of your thinking. You will learn simple strategies to increase energy levels and remove the biochemical causes of many emotions. This section will be invaluable for both you and your family. I have learned through long years of clinical practice that the biochemical "fog" in which many people live makes change almost impossible. You may think that your thought processes are clear. Perhaps they are, but don't skip this section—you will gain great benefits from it, even if only to understand the "odd" behaviour of others around you.

Then we begin to analyse the specifics of Neuro-Com, showing you the structure of the language your unconscious mind uses to communicate with you. You will conduct some experiments to learn and understand your mind's "accent." Just as different people speak with different accents, your mind also has its own tones and colour to its language. Your mind is unique; you should find it easy to recognise its patterns.

Chapter 5 begins to set up your future by drawing up what I have chosen to call *NeuroPrints*. NeuroPrints are simply mental blueprints or plans that incorporate Neuro-Com into their design. In other words, we create a future plan, which uses your unconscious mind's language. In this way, your mind can understand your orders clearly and embed their consequences in your future.

Further chapters put your future plan in place on which your mind can act. Then we come back to the present and show you how to understand someone else's Neuro-Com patterns so that you can give your mind an order to create a certain type of relationship with someone else. Your mind will evaluate the other person's patterns automatically and use them to get what you want. Let me repeat this and ensure you understand the implications!

"Then we come back to the present and show you how to understand someone else's Neuro-Com patterns so that you can give your mind an order to create a certain type of relationship with someone else. It will evaluate the other person's patterns automatically and use them to get what you want."

What I'm saying is that you can program your unconscious mind to communicate with others at an unconscious level and create an outcome that is in your interest. Think what this means in relationships: for sales people or for anyone who relies on interacting with other people. In

The Neuro-Com Program

personal relationships, including parental and social, such unconscious congruency enhances the experience and allows natural and fulfilling connections to be developed. If you extend this understanding to larger relationships, such as groups, religions, and nations, you may begin to understand that there is potential to reprogram the direction in which the human race is headed.

If you are involved in any kind of job or business that involves dealing with people, you will find this program exceptionally helpful. I have had great success training groups involved in sales and multi-level marketing businesses with these strategies to create substantial success. Using these strategies, you can eliminate the fear of talking to people and establish rapport with anyone you wish.

Chapter 8 ties together everything you have learned during the course and provides a direction for further developing the principles in your life and in the lives of those around you. It's kind of like a computer being given its own intelligent program whereby it begins to learn on its own, possibly far exceeding the original knowledge provided. Once the old shackles are discarded from your mind, you begin to realise your full potential and can far exceed your current view of the world. Chapter 8 also discusses the elusive concept of happiness.

I wish you every success, both with the program and with the amazing results you can achieve with it.

HOW TO USE THIS PROGRAM

If you have received this program in an electronic format, either via the email distribution system or on disc media, you will need to print it first. The program includes many forms on which you will need to write, and you may need several copies of each form. The book has been formatted for easy distribution, which makes some of the forms you need difficult to use. For this reason, you have access to downloadable versions of the forms available for printing at www.neuro-com.org. Please note that apart from duplicating the forms, you are only permitted to print one copy of the program for your own use. You must not distribute the program to your friends.

Make Notes as You Go

This entire program is designed around PRACTICAL CHANGE techniques. It is important that you recognise how the ideas we discuss **apply to you**. The best way to do this is to make notes as you progress through the program. Trying to remember ideas that will pop into your mind is a waste of time in most cases. Your unconscious mind will sit up and take more notice of your intentions if it knows you are participating actively.

Jot down plenty of notes as you go: in the margins, in a note book, wherever you can. This book is designed to be used in a very practical way. Not making notes in the book just tells your unconscious mind that the way the book looks is more important than you and your future. Is it? In addition, I suggest you buy a special notebook that has a feel of quality and importance, in which you will enter your thoughts about how the Neuro-Com process can be seen in the way you think and behave, both individually and in your interactions with others. Many of the exercises you will find through the book will also ask you to make notes on these interactions.

Work the exercises

As you move through each chapter, please take the time to work through the exercises presented. Some of the activity will appear strange to you initially. As you get accustomed to the idea of communicating with your unconscious, you will start to see some events in your life that confirm that your mind is taking notice. When this starts to happen, you will believe the system works, and it will become even more powerful for you.

Make sure you set aside time in your schedule to work through the exercises so you develop a clear understanding of the principles behind them. More important, ensure you understand how YOU are reacting and the way your conscious mind is reading your unconscious thought and feeling reactions. I will explain more of what I mean by this at the appropriate point. For now, however, make the commitment to yourself that you will expend the needed energy. Remember, your unconscious mind is watching and will take your lead as to how important the issues are for you. It is asking for your instructions.

Don't skip any chapters

Using the Neuro-Com strategies described in subsequent chapters requires you to think clearly. Through long experience, I have found that about 30% of people in Western populations suffer from biochemical imbalances serious enough to cause cloudy or slow thinking. Chapter 2 covers ways to remove any physical limitations to change.

You may be tempted to skip this chapter if you think you are not affected, but I ask you not to do so. While you may be quite right in assessing your state, it is important for later chapters that you understand the state others around you may occupy. Such states will affect the way others interact with you and, as a result, will almost certainly affect your emotions and the direction of your life.

The programming you have taken on board, the emotional content of your memory, and the decisions in memory all have a level of energetic input. Changing such content requires expending energy through the energy of **directed thought**. If you find you need to modify your diet, spend the time and energy to do it. The hours you take to make changes will be the most valuable hours of your entire life.

If you don't take the work seriously, neither will your unconscious mind.

Important!

At some time during the program, you will almost certainly feel some resistance from your unconscious. This is normal. At times, you will probably find everything else in the world will become more important than completing a chapter or an exercise. If you walk away at that moment, you will confirm to your unconscious that the behaviours it provides to you are correct. Please remember, YOU are the controller. Resist the temptation to be distracted.

If the processes in which you engage during the exercises produce a serious negative reaction of high anxiety or panic, STOP. This will usually only occur if you have severe trauma in your background that remains unresolved. Your mind is making you aware that you are treading on uncomfortable ground and is actually trying to protect you by creating emotional upheaval. As you will find by reading through the program, your unconscious mind frequently creates behaviours to protect you, but it does not understand that the behaviours it is using may also be causing you more trauma. In a clinical setting, this is resolved easily. Quite often, I work with people long distance to resolve such traumas and do so with a great deal of success.

You will notice that certain concepts or phrases are repeated throughout the program. Your unconscious program will pick these out and take more notice of them. This is an important part of the process. Be patient.

THE NEURO-COM WEBSITE

Many questions will pass across your mind. Perhaps some things will appear difficult. Perhaps you just need to get someone else's ideas. We have setup a support website to help.

The Neuro-Com Program

Go to **www.neuro-com.org**. You will find sections on Frequently Asked Questions, Information Updates, Contact Information, and downloadable information files in PDF format on related topics.

As you progress through the book you will find several forms that are an essential part of the program for you to complete. Because the book's format makes it difficult to create forms in a useful size, all the forms are available for you to download from the website's Download folders. They are in PDF format so you will need a copy of Acrobat Reader to open them. This is a free application; most computers these days already have PDF readers installed. If you don't, however, full instructions are included on the website.

On the website you will also find information about me and ways to contact me.

Above all, please enjoy the experience. Creating change in your mind may sometimes seem like a daunting task. Most people find it difficult using "normal" techniques because such techniques don't take into account the mind chatter that occurs between the conscious and unconscious mind. As you become accustomed to being the controller and being conscious of your thought and feeling reactions, you will find that controlling your environment and the people in it will be simple and easy.

Enjoy your journey.

CHAPTER ONE

Human Drives and Limiters

> **This chapter discusses:**
>
> ❖ The Global Problem
>
> ❖ The difference between success, mediocrity, and failure
>
> ❖ The difference between a peaceful existence and stress-filled hell
>
> ❖ The enigma of emotional memory
>
> ❖ Memory groups, self-image, and personality
>
> ❖ Human interaction and communication
>
> ❖ Relationships
>
> ❖ The 6 Ds: First Steps on the Path

THE GLOBAL PROBLEM

Most people on this planet Earth, thanks to the speed of communications and saturated advertising, seek greater wealth and worldly goods. Most often, they find that those riches and worldly goods elude them or cost far more in emotional turmoil than was anticipated. Despite all this, very few succeed in finding their Utopia. Time and time again, we hear from the wealthy that their wealth did not bring them happiness.

Frustration and anger abound. Stress levels in society are escalating at an alarming rate. The medical costs that result are helping to bankrupt entire countries. In Australia, the cost can be counted in many billions, although the research often attributes these disease states to other causes. In my years of clinical practice, I have proven that teaching people the tools to reduce levels of anxiety significantly improves their overall health and often eliminates disease states.

For many, the future appears very dark indeed. Yet the answers are here, right now. Societies' problems can be solved through some incredibly simple understandings. The problems of stress and health, fear, anger, guilt, and anxiety can all be eliminated.

It all begins with YOU simply taking responsibility for **YOU**. You do not need to go out and save the world, scoring brownie points for the afterlife. Jesus Christ is recorded as having made several pleas for us to solve our own problems before going out to save the world. *"First remove the plank from your own eye so that you can see clearly to take the speck from your brother's."*

You may well be challenged by some of the methods of becoming aware of your own internal experience. Treat such challenges as a wonderful learning experience. If you can get excited about each new discovery, do so. The new energy of excitement is powerful in your communication with your unconscious mind.

The journey you are about to take will lead you to the mountaintop. From there you will be able to see far beyond your normal horizons. You will be able to see past the nearby cliff faces to the beautiful and peaceful valleys beyond. Choose now to enjoy your journey to the mountaintop. And, when you have reached the peak you may choose to be like the eagle, soaring far above the highest physical states. When you chose to achieve such heights, you can see all the way to infinity!

SUCCESS, MEDIOCRITY, AND FAILURE

You have been programmed! Today, at this moment, you are doing exactly what you have been programmed to do. Very few individuals have the skills required to break out of that programming. Using our new understanding of how the mind communicates, however, YOU can choose to take your life into you own hands and create the kind of life YOU want to live.

It is no longer "okay" to allow a large part of the human race to suffer anxiety, fear, guilt, and anger inflicted by those in authority over us from the moment we are born. The programming our societies has inflicted on us is having horrific results. And, at the risk of offending, the religions have been a major purveyor of guilt, anxiety, and traumas that continue to inflict their pain on groups and individuals.

Every one of us took on an unconscious program during our early years. Unless you have taken deliberate steps to reverse this program, it still controls your every behaviour. The people and events around you were indelibly imprinted into your unconscious memory in an effort to create a protective barrier to dangerous behaviour. Your view of what is "normal" is determined by that recording. Even the way you see, hear, and feel your world around you is modified by the "accent" created by your program.

Your ability to create a lifestyle, income, friendships, and other relationships is controlled and limited by the information, circumstances, and subliminal input with which you have been programmed. **The very people who thought they were protecting you did most of the damage in your first five to seven years of life!**

Clinical practice had shown that individuals who exhibit high levels of anxiety and distress often come from families who lived amidst tension and verbal or physical violence. In general, the higher the level of distress, the more energy has been recorded in the personal memory.

Statistics show that 90% of people suffering from the extremes of mental illness come from backgrounds that contain anger, violence, or extreme guilt. Seventy per cent of patients in mental institutions suffer from PTSD (post-traumatic stress disorder), which results from being exposed to severe violence or death.

Furthermore, both men and women suffer from incredible sexual conflict. Levels of anger, both at an individual level and at a community level, are increasing. Internal self-image conflicts and guilt about being

The Neuro-Com Program

successful are now causing millions of people to stop trying to change their life for the better.

Please do not grab the telephone to call your parents and grandparents to heap abuse on them for the programming they have given you. In most cases they had no other way to deal with their situation. They behaved toward you and spoke to you in a way that was in turn based on how they were programmed by those in authority over them when they were children. Unless they had access to the skills you will soon learn and did something about their programs, they had no more control over their thoughts and behaviours than you currently do.

It is your responsibility to feel the way you want and create what you desire from now on.

The time has come for massive change. Humankind can no longer afford to carry the imposed stresses and strains of living in a sick society. The cost in human suffering of living within the restrictions of social disharmony is now causing states of personal disharmony and disease that can only lead to the disintegration of society.

For thousands of years, populations have been battered into conformity. The individual and high achiever, while publicly a desired breed, has been brought down to the level of others simply by long-term programming. Very few of us really believe that we deserve to achieve beyond the norm. When we do create such achievements, we often sabotage ourselves, with our programming creating the behaviours that ensure our failure!

Over the years, I have asked dozens of public audiences the same question: "Who believes that most of the people in this room are better than you in most things—better in looks, more intelligent, or have a better personality?" The sad thing is that more than 95 per cent of the average audience will raise their hand to this question. The irony is that those we believe are better than us usually feel we are better than they are in some way. Is either right?

You may not be able to do a great deal to change the entire human race, but you can change the way you react to your environment, your personal emotions, and the way you feel about yourself. You can change the way you view the future. The time has come for you to throw off the chains of your social and personal programming.

We now have powerful tools to do this. Over the past fifteen years, we have developed new tools to dramatically enhance your control over your emotions and the amazing creative power of your mind.

The Neuro-Com program will teach you those tools. It will give you resources you may have only dreamed about in the past:

- Resources to completely rid yourself of stress and anxiety.
- Resources to create a future for you and your family you have never thought possible.
- Resources to take back your power and choose how you want to lead your life!

THE POWERFUL MECHANISM OF "NOW"

The most misused catch-cry of the past 40 years is "Live in NOW."

To discover how to do this, millions of "truth" seekers have latched onto mystical gurus and religions seeking enlightenment and freedom—usually without an understanding of what enlightenment actually means.

Tens of thousands sit cross-legged on mountaintops trying to meditate to understand reality, having been told by their guru that this life and all that surrounds them is a dream. Bookshops are filled with thousands of books on the subject of self-development and the way to perfect enlightenment. Millions seek the truth through New Age thinking, visualisation, affirmations, crystals, mystics, and a thousand other beliefs. Hundreds of millions more seek a more peaceful existence; free of the ghosts from the past and memories and emotions with which they have lived for decades.

I know I'll incur the wrath of many for saying this. but I am going to say it anyway. In our society, the psychiatrists, psychologists, and other mental health professionals often make a fortune by following the closed belief that emotional change takes months or years to achieve. It is not unusual for the medical benefits system to pay tens of thousands of dollars to try to help a single individual, often with little or no result.

If real change takes a long time to create, why have I consistently— over the past 35 years—been able to remove the depths of trauma from people who have suffered from post-traumatic stress disorder and other anxiety disorders for decades within just a couple of hours? Many of these clients have been Vietnam vets, emergency services workers, and victims of rape or natural disasters. They have been taken down the traditional treatment paths for years or decades, gradually getting worse, until they become suicidal. Yet using a simple model of the mind and specially developed techniques, their overwhelming anxiety, fear, depression, and anger can be eliminated quickly and with perfect safety.

Millions of people every year pay hard-earned money to the gurus of the "personal development" industry. Many get no results. The ones that do experience a difference through "hot bath motivation" techniques soon revert to old behaviours, because they are never taught how to defuse the emotional content or the limiting decisions their mind has made in the past.

Please understand I am not criticising *individuals*, only *the system* that forces them to work within a closely defined view of mental health. There are now far more powerful understandings of the mind with a complete set of strategies to use as tools for change. Change can often be instant, as you will soon find. I have used these simple strategies to remove lifelong phobias within a few minutes and remove traumatic flashbacks of those suffering decades of post-traumatic stress disorder— in seconds.

The secret to your ability to create massive change lies in simplicity. You see, you can't produce anything in the future. You will find that the past does not exist except in memory and can have no power over you unless you choose, either actively or by neglect, to give it power. We typically abdicate responsibility for our behaviours—the way we treat others and talk to them and most important the way we feel—to our unconscious programs. In doing so, we blame our parents, our teachers, our religions, and our governments for the state of our existence. In reality, most of us live in the past, overwhelmed by our emotional and experiential memory.

Change can only occur NOW, and NOW is about as simple as anything can be. Your thoughts *in this moment* create your life, your relationships and your level of success. You experience your emotions NOW. You experience your joys, your fears, and your behaviours NOW. There is nothing simpler than this moment in time.

By understanding how your energetic memory works, you will be able to understand how to change your enjoyment of life and how to create an amazing future for yourself. This program is designed to give you the resources to do just that.

That wonderful old catch-cry "Live in NOW!" has a great deal of power behind it. But to actually do it is not as easy as it sounds. You are going to learn how to do it by eliminating the reactive thoughts and feelings driven by past memory. You will learn what true harmony and spirituality really are and how they can be achieved.

The Six D's: The First Steps on the Path

If your life is not as you want it and the door to your future appears to be closed and locked, you must understand one thing as clearly as a perfect diamond. YOU are the only key that will open the door.

Up to this point in your life, you may have blamed your parents for your misfortune. Perhaps it has been the teachers with whom you were inflicted. Or that bully in grade 5 who gave you a hard time. Or do you blame your current circumstances? It is not unusual for us to place the blame for our circumstances on our government. It is, after all, the government that creates or destroys prosperity within a society. If you can't get a job or you earn less than you believe you should, it is easy to blame your life's circumstances.

The Neuro-Com Program

Look at it realistically. Why do others get paid more? Why do others seem to have the lifestyle you would like? Why do a select few seem to have everything go well for them? Do you think it is because they just happened to be in the right place at the right time? They just happened to go to the right schools?

Yes, for some these things are true. Some have come from well-structured families and have been taught some self-discipline. Some have had the opportunity to have above-average teachers and other role models. Some have been just lucky.

The reality is that those who get the best have made themselves more valuable to the marketplace. They have spent time developing their own knowledge and skills. In some cases they have spent time and energy removing their own internal fears and uncertainties. They have expended energy developing the contacts they needed. They have moved out of their comfort zone to foster the kind of life that they desired.

In short, they have taken responsibility for themselves!

We all need to do the same. This program will give you the most powerful methods of change ever created by the human mind. However unless you **take responsibility** for your life from this moment on, such methods of change are rendered useless. Every now and then, I have a client come into the clinic who makes it clear that my role is to change the world around him or her! I must quickly make them aware that no one can do that. They can only change themselves and take responsibility for how they view their environment and the people around them.

There are some basic rules we must follow to make lasting change for the better. I like to refer to these simply as "The 6 Ds of Personal Power." They are:

- Decision
- Desire
- Direction
- Discipline
- Determination
- Daily Method of Operation

1. DECISION

The word DECISION is one of the most powerful words in the English language. Without it, nothing is created. No one begins any endeavour without first making a decision, a mental note, that it is time to begin NOW. Time to take the first step, to begin work, to write the first word. Without a decision, buildings never get built, nations never grow, and individuals never change. For you to create anything new in your life, you must make the decision to change what you are doing now and allow new strategies and people to enter your life. This does not mean that you need to discard everything of your past. I'm sure your partner in life, if you have one, might take exception to that idea!

It does mean that you need to open your mind to new ways of doing things and give your unconscious mind permission to take on some new behaviour, thinking patterns, and attitudes about your ability to create a successful life *according to the design you consciously wish to implement*. For this to happen, a **decision** to begin acts as an instruction to your unconscious mind that a new path is to be taken seriously.

One of my mentors often repeated his definition of insanity:

"Insanity is doing the things you have always done, in the same way you have always done them, and expecting the outcome to be different!"

Make the DECISION now to be responsible for your life from the point on! What you do now will determine the direction of your future.

Exercise – Your Life Manual

In the next 24 hours make time to go to a stationer or bookshop and buy a blank book. I don't mean a loose-leaf folder of spiral-bound paper. I mean a permanently bound blank book with a cover that feels and looks valuable. There are many available, some with ruled lines, some totally blank. Your selection should not be based on price but on its quality, look, and feel and how you react to it. It should look and feel valuable and say to you "I'm yours".

This Learning Journal will become your Life Manual—your design for your future life in all its aspects. It will give you clarity in your plans for the way you feel and act. It will give your unconscious mind its instructions to plan your relationships, health, income, and recreation. It will guide your spiritual evolution if you so desire. This notebook will become your understanding of how your unconscious mind communicates with you and how you command it to behave and feel differently. It is fluid canvas on which you will paint your imagination and make it real.

It has always fascinated me how most people spend more time planning their next holiday than in planning their long-term future. Perhaps it is because we don't feel as if we have control over our future. True, the influence of and interaction with other people often directs and changes our life's circumstances. But this is mostly because our unconscious mind selects the people in our life based on information with which it has been programmed as being suitable relationships, business partners, and lovers. As you will find, these programs can be changed so that your unconscious brings you to relationships with others that are supportive, creative, and productive. Hence, when you use your Life Manual to design your future, you will be creating a very different future based on instructions that you will be providing your unconscious programs. And so, we begin!

Sit down and read the statement that follows. Spend several minutes putting some emotional energy into YOUR DECISION to be responsible for your future. Think about your past and the aspects of your present you wish to change. Understand the fact that you are where you are now in life because of the program you have accepted unconsciously in the past. If you need to do so, get angry about your past, yourself, or anything else that has limited you. Create a passion to change.

Then turn to the front page of your journal and write:

> "I, (insert your full name), now make the irrevocable DECISION to take responsibility for my future in all aspects of my life."

Take your time and be careful how you write it. Take pride in what you are doing, like an artist starting a new painting with all the love and care that this entails. You are doing this for YOU. This is the beginning of a new life that YOU control. You have started to instruct your unconscious mind that the strategies you are beginning to teach it are to be taken seriously.

Now sign your statement and date it.

Use your journal to note all of the important aspects of your life and the most important things you learn from this program. This will become your learning journal.

2. DESIRE

The second of the 6 Ds is DESIRE. To create any outcome, there must first be the desire to create. As you will discover when we discuss the way your mind really works, the level of emotional energy you put into any endeavour will determine how much attention your unconscious mind gives it.

Desire is totally different from NEED or WANT. You can want something but not be too worried if you don't achieve it. You can need something, but that need may not be enough to get you off your behind and go and do something about it. Without upsetting too many people, I will use a common situation in society worldwide as an example—the unemployed.

I have been involved with several business ventures in varied market areas, both as an employee, then as an owner, and later as a business consultant. In every situation, one thing becomes obvious over and over again—*"some will and some won't."* Those people who want or need a job rarely have the drive to give value to money. They are generally happy to drift through life, working on ways to get the most out of the boss for the minimum amount of work. The WANT or NEED is not enough to stimulate independent activity. Those who want or need a job may get one, but rarely excel or move into anything that requires responsibility of self-motivation, such as starting a business. The only things that are valuable to the market place are activity and value. It takes more than want or need to drive these.

DESIRE is a different story. Even the sound of the word holds energy! Have you ever wanted something so much your internal organs ached?

I remember when I just a kid of nine years old. I had been to a go-cart track with some friends of my parents and had experienced the exhilaration of whizzing around the track at what seemed like death-defying speeds. The feeling of the wind in my face and the blurred view of the passing world was an experience I have never forgotten. Perhaps that's why I now tend to drive far faster than I should!

That one day in my life created an emotion I had never felt before, and it carried with it such power that it was irresistible—D E S I R E!

I had to have a go-cart! I plotted, schemed, and manipulated my parents into getting me one of these excitement machines. I used every one of my very limited social skills to make my parents (and any other possible financial backer who happened to stroll across my predatory path) buy one. I even made promises to wash the dishes for the rest of my life. That's desperate!

The energy paid off. Christmas day in my ninth year saw the DESIRE finally become reality. My handy father and his mate had spent long hours building one for me. Sure, it didn't have a motor, but going downhill it was the fastest thing on wheels. Without the DESIRE, I would never have created awareness in other people to provide it. If I had merely wanted it or needed it, I would not have had the emotional power to create it.

Understand this point clearly. If you are not creating the life you want, there are two things you must do to create a different future. First, determine what kind of lifestyle you would like to live. In other words, create some goals as targets toward which you will head. We will cover the creation of Neuro-Dynamically Effective (NDE) goals in a subsequent chapter.

Second, you must create a powerful DESIRE to bring YOUR GOALS to reality. Sometimes, you will find it difficult to create desire, and a huge difference will exist between consciously desiring something and the outcome you will eventually achieve. This is because your value system may be in opposition to your NOW desire. Such conflicts are easily removed, as you will soon see when we look at your VALUES system and how it influences your life.

3. DIRECTION

I think it was Mickey Mouse who first made the profound observation, *"If you don't know where you are going, you'll probably end up someplace else!"*

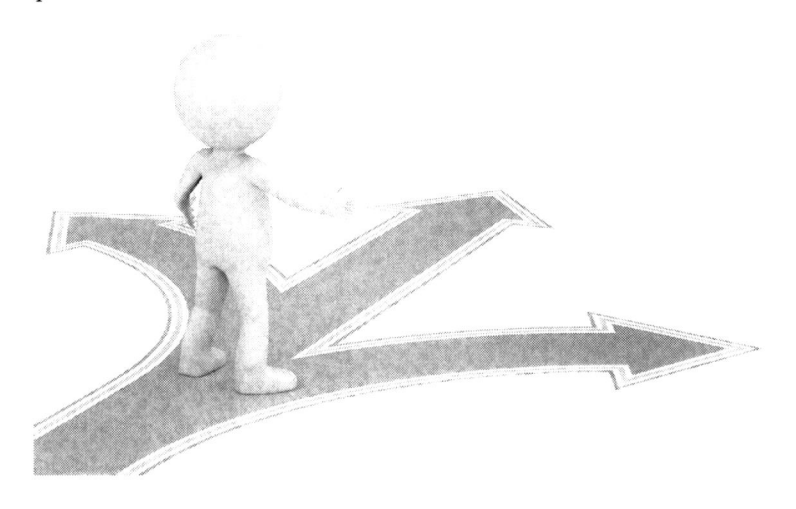

The Neuro-Com Program

It's easy to lose our way in life. We are assaulted by a billion unconscious stimulations a day. The demands on us, physically and mentally, are increasing annually. Day-to-day demands make us concentrate on the things that are critical to us right now and force us to forget why we are doing the job in the first place. There is an old adage that sometimes we spend so much of our time fighting the crocodiles that we forget the original goal was to drain the swamp!

The result? We lose focus on the important things—the reasons "why" we are doing things. **We spend major time on doing minor things.** As a result, the vast majority of us never achieve anything significant in life. Reality has been shown us time and time again that 80% of our productivity results from only 20% of our activity. What would happen if you could focus so that 40% of your activity was directed at productivity? You would produce 200% more effective output than you do now! You would achieve this not by working harder but by focusing on things that really matter. By using 60% of your time in a productive way, you would produce 300% more output than you do now. In many cases the only change you need to make is in planning your time a little better.

It is critical that we have a clear direction in which to head. We create that direction by expending energy in developing a life plan, weaving it with all the care that goes into a beautiful Persian rug. Without such a life plan, your unconscious behaviours will always conform to the old limiting program. With a life plan, you can have anything you want.

Your life plan needs to be created in a specific way that will alert your unconscious mind to sit up and take notice. The method we use to do this is what I call a **NeuroPrint**. It acts as a new program, a map to guide your unconscious mind. The prime characteristic of a NeuroPrint is that it is emotionally congruent with your values system. If you want something that seems outside your current values system at an unconscious level, then the process of creating your NeuroPrint also modifies or adds a new value.

Many years ago I developed a personal development program called The Success Skills Program. I taught the program to thousands of people looking to make a difference in their lives. In the many years of presenting program, I found only a handful of people who had really put any effort into designing their life. Most, not realising the importance of creating DIRECTION, had spent their entire life bumping along the bottom, being turned here and there by circumstances and other people. They never planned anything more than a few months ahead, and they had no concept of the controlling influence of their unconscious mind and the programs it runs.

When we give people the precise tools with which to create their life plan and specific goals, their goals begin to be created almost immediately! You will engage in several exercises in this program to begin to weave your own life plan.

Do not be lax in your efforts here. The hours you invest in the exercise will repay you a thousand times over. Those hours may make the difference between a life of misery and mediocrity or a life of health, wealth, and recognition.

Believe me—the view from the top is colourful and crystal clear. You can see a thousand times farther from the vantage point of an eagle than you can from the vantage point of a field mouse, the eagle's prey!

We will look into how to create DIRECTION using your own personal NeuroPrint in a later chapter.

4. DISCIPLINE

So now you have your goals set and associated values in place. The next of the 6 Ds that must be addressed is DISCIPLINE. Here I do not mean having the headmaster rap you over the knuckles as a stimulus to better performance. I'm talking about SELF-DISCIPLINE.

Self-discipline is a rarity in ordinary people. And, let's face it, the vast majority of our society is, and always will be, ordinary. The fact that you are reading this now probably indicates that you are no longer happy to be part of the ordinary 97%.

A major difference between the 97% and the 3% of which you want to be a part is the magic of self-discipline. So, it is important to understand exactly what self-discipline is and why it is so powerful.

The Neuro-Com Program

Your unconscious conditioning creates a large proportion of your behaviours and drives. The beliefs and learning you took on board during that first critical five years of life determine your needs and wants, and even your desires, on a daily basis. Your unconscious mind, untempered by conscious input, will provide you with emotional reactions and behaviours appropriate for what it "thinks" are okay now. These behaviours will often move you away from activities you should be doing by making other jobs or pleasures more important to you.

I see this, and experience it, on a daily basis. In sales and marketing, the need to talk to others creates one of the greatest fears and limiting behaviours. This obviously allows the phantom of a "NO" to rear its ugly head. No one likes rejection, and the fear of rejection typically reduces the average salesperson to 20% efficiency!

To protect you from this crippling fear, your unconscious mind will find at least a million things that appear more important than picking up the phone or going out to see a client. The car needs cleaning, or you have to do some paperwork, or you have to have another cup of coffee, or it's raining too hard, or the cat ate the budgie, or....

Anything will do. And, your mind can amplify the importance of such activities so that you don't even become aware you are engaging in avoidance behaviour. The same avoidance behaviour comes into play when you must talk with someone with whom you've had an argument or someone you regard with over-awing respect.

The answer is SELF-DISCIPLINE. Become aware of your behaviours. Become a student of you. The very precise tools you will learn in this manual will show you how. Then you must expend energy to consciously change your behaviours. That conscious energy is SELF-DISCIPLINE. It's about taking charge of your behaviour and taking responsibility.

Let me make one final point on this topic of discipline. It is a good idea to ask yourself, *"What is the difference between someone without discipline and someone who displays self-discipline in everything they do?"* As a keen observer of people and behaviour, I have become acutely aware that those who have the great skill of self-discipline are usually those who received discipline in their younger years, especially the first five years. Why is this so? I believe it is because when we are disciplined we learn two things. The first thing we learn is that others have a role in our life and that there are consequences for being self-focussed. The second thing we learn is that we become accustomed to doing things we may not particularly like to do. Both of these stand us in good stead later. People without these skills tend to think only of themselves and how the world affects them. We will discuss the effects of this on success and happiness later.

5. DETERMINATION

One of the most powerful strategies in the self-discipline armoury is DETERMINATION. Determination is self-discipline with a time-directed focus. That is, DETERMINATION implies completion or finality and therefore has an end point. "I am determined to......" always has a goal or target in mind. Consequently, it is perhaps the easiest of the 6 Ds to infuse with enthusiasm and energy. Short-term goals can often be completed without developing conscious strategies of energy infusion. They often do not require sustained determination. Medium- to long-term goals are a totally different story. Very few of us can maintain enthusiasm long enough to complete such conscious targets because there are almost always interferences in the process. Other things come into conscious awareness that appear more important or are easier to complete. In many cases of a consciously desirable outcome, your unconscious mind, because of its energetic program, will divert your attention. It doesn't believe you should have the outcome you consciously want! Again, such behaviour is typically driven by early unconscious self-image programming.

Remember the last time you had to get your affairs in order for the annual tax return? Or there was some other job you had to do, but didn't want to do—perhaps painting your mother-in-law's house? If you are like most of us, a million other things seemed more important, and you kept putting the job off. It's normal for us to avoid things we don't want to do.

There is only one way to counter-balance the vagaries of day-to-day interference. Create a personal energetic strategy of

DETERMINATION. We'll discuss exactly how to enhance your level of DETERMINATION a hundred-fold in our discussion on modifying values. If your unconscious mind is congruent with the goal you require determination to complete, then the whole process becomes automatic rather than a struggle.

6. DAILY METHOD OF OPERATION

So now we have made the DECISION to create change. We have the DESIRE to change and have created the DIRECTION in which we wish to head. We have developed the (self-) DISCIPLINE to ensure we do the things that are necessary to create the change and the DETERMINATION to allow us to follow through to completion.

The last of the 6 Ds is DAILY METHOD OF OPERATION. All of the above has been directed at "the big picture," the master plan of change and final outcome. We now need the hand tools with which to fashion the master plan. Those tools are the details of your DAILY METHOD OF OPERATION or DMO. Developing a DMO allows you to take steps of a manageable size, each step leading you to your ultimate destination. In reality, your DMO is a step-by-step design of your NeuroPrint or life plan.

Have you ever heard the old saying: "You can eat an elephant, one bite at a time"? Or another, equally as true, "The longest journey begins with the first step." These truisms imply you can make it easy for your unconscious mind to accept change initially, but you need to give it some minor daily successes to prove to it that the succeeding journey is viable. And, change is not only viable, but congruently desirable! We will provide proven tools to set your personal DMO in place.

Remember the Rule

There are certain things you must do, that we could perhaps call Rules or Laws, which must be in place or active before change can occur. This is especially true in the way we live our lives. History has demonstrated that the people who succeed in living a fulfilling life tend to follow such guiding Rules, whether they are aware of it or not.

Human Drives and Limiters

The First Law of Life Enhancement demands you put energy into creating change in those areas of life and belief that do not currently support your desired outcomes.

Do not be mentally or physically lazy in understanding and implementing the strategies and exercises presented here. I am always amazed at the number of people who go to work and evidently work 40 hours per week or more, mostly in jobs they don't like. And yet, they can't find time to expend a couple of hours per week to design their future. As I have said, most people put more energy and forethought into planning their annual holiday than in planning a successful life for themselves and their family.

If you are one of these people and are unwilling to expend the energy to design the kind of life you really want, close this book now and give it to someone who truly desires a greater future. Watch their progress. When you are finally convinced that these strategies work in the most powerful way, and understand that so few hours are worth so much, get another copy and begin again.

Or, make the DECISION NOW to follow this program through to completion.

Why do so many people fail to create what they want through personal development or change programs? Your mind stores emotional energy. It will generally be influenced more heavily by memory and strategies that have been recorded with a high level of emotional charge. As groups of similar memories are recorded and encoded, they tend to combine the levels of energy, either negative or positive. In the next section, I will discuss how this happens. But for now, it is enough to understand it this way.

You are driving a 20-tonne truck down a straight highway. This could represent your pre-programmed unconscious memory system. The road is littered with potholes and other disturbances; the steering wheel shakes and shimmers as the wheels find these potholes. Still, the 20-tonne truck will almost always continue on its original path. The truck's kinetic energy will maintain its original direction UNLESS you put considerable energy into changing its direction. To veer to the left or right a little doesn't take much. This is the usual level of energy and determination we put into changing our lives. Our mind finds it easy to come back to the old course. But what happens if we want to turn off onto a completely different road, a crossroad? Have you ever seen a truck driver struggle with the steering wheel and put in some hard work? Once he or she has turned the corner and is heading in a straight path again, the task is once again easy.

Your mind works the same way. If you put effort into making a SIGNIFICANT change in direction, your unconscious mind will see it as a new program, totally unrelated to the old one, and you will easily be able to maintain course.

But here's the catch. Your unconscious memory system has a specific way of communicating with the outside world. Furthermore, its method is generally specific to YOU as an individual. To communicate with it effectively and have it change direction, you must understand how it expects to be addressed and have the tools to negotiate new behaviours.

CHAPTER TWO

How Your Mind Really Works

> **This chapter discusses:**
>
> - Conscious and unconscious mind
> - The first five years: Original root cause memory
> - The basis of beliefs
> - Evolvement of values: Emotional coherence
> - Belief and values conflicts
> - Attitude and its resultant behaviour
> - Your timeline and its role in your future

You are probably not in control of your behaviour, emotions, or day-to-day thoughts. A part of your mind, often termed your unconscious or subconscious mind, controls the vast majority of behaviour and communication. And it often does so based on incorrect or incomplete information!

It is important to understand the function of the different parts of your mind, along with their powers and limitations. There are literally thousands of books available discussing how the mind works. There have been hundreds of practitioners and writers who claim to have an accurate description of how the mind works. Some have part of it right. Some are totally off track.

The representation I am about to present is based on practical experience and a simple fact. The fact is that everyone who uses the strategies on which this book is based achieves clear, positive results. This is because this work recognises that YOUR mind is unique and has its own Life Direction Pattern.

Your Life Direction Pattern is the patterns that automatically exist in behaviours, thoughts and feelings that direct the way you interact with and how you communicate with others. It also determines what actions you take to create the direction your life heads in at all stages of experience. In other words, your Life Direction Pattern determines how your life pans out.

No one else has the same programs and Life Direction Patterns you have, and the variations on the theme of mental strategies we have are numerous. The model you are about to learn is based on more than 35 years of intense clinical experience that has involved a very wide field of human experience. It becomes even more critical to have an accurate model when dealing with extremes in anxiety disorders and mental illness, understanding the basis and evolution of distress, love and laughter.

Let's begin by looking at the apparent structure of the "base" mind. For the sake of this manual, we will consider only two components of the mind—the conscious and the unconscious.

THE CONSCIOUS MIND—GATEWAY TO NOW

Raise your right hand above your head and hold it there for a few seconds. Then return it to its former location. Did you do that with your conscious awareness? The answer is no. And yes.

"No" because you did not make individual adjustments to each of the muscles and nerves in your arm. You did not consciously convert the stored reserves of chemical energy to the energy required by the thousands of nerves and dozens of muscles to create the movement. You cannot process more than a few different thoughts at a time using your conscious mind. It would take considerable time to run through the processes to move your arm in that manner with any degree of smoothness. So, it was not your conscious mind that physically made your hand move. Consider a more complex requirement of moving from where you are now to walking out to your post box and back. That process requires literally thousands of tiny processes to occur at the levels of body biochemistry, nervous system, and organ and muscle movements in order to complete the task. If you had to do this consciously it would take you days or weeks to perform a simple task.

However, "yes" is also a correct answer because you did give your unconscious mind an instruction. That instruction came in the form of a vague visual memory of what your arm looks like to have your hand in that position—or an awareness of how your arm feels to be in that position. In the case of walking to the post box, you created an image of actually getting to the post box and back. That simple, conscious thought became the instruction for your unconscious mind to use its vast resources to supply the correct amount of energy to the muscles. It provided the nerve stimulation that caused each of your muscles to contract, each one by the appropriate amount and at the appropriate time with split-second precision.

Consider the millions of unconscious processes that go into the complex act of driving a car! Yet you can not only drive, but you often do it without any conscious input at all. When was the last time you remembered every part of a road trip accurately? In the case of a road trip to a familiar destination, all you do is picture the final destination. All the past learning your unconscious has done then takes over and runs the automated programs to get you there.

It works as though your unconscious memory stores thousands of individual programs, each one being able to trigger others. In the example just given, hundreds of processes are performed at the same time, but it takes only a single conscious instruction to trigger the mechanism.

Think of it in terms of a computer that you may be using for a dozen different functions. For example, when you use a word processor, you typically only use the mouse to click an icon on the desktop relating to that program. This is the equivalent of you beginning the chain of events with a single command from your conscious mind. Once that command is initiated, dozens—or even hundreds—of small programs go into action to start the program, create the screen design, set up the word processor's tools and templates, and so on. All of this goes on in the background, and you are not even aware of it. So it is with your mind.

If you are going to begin taking control of your life, you must understand how your mind is functioning. From there you work out the strategies YOU need to use to change your behaviours and communication. It is these unique strategies that will become powerful allies in creating the kind of life you really would like.

Most of us mistakenly think we are our conscious mind and that we are in control. In fact, your conscious mind is simply your awareness of what is happening around you, and within you, **at this moment in time**. As such, it is your conscious mind that has the power to instruct your unconscious mind, and **it is your conscious mind that has the power to create**.

Each of your senses—sight, sound, smell, taste and touch— contributes information to your awareness of the events occurring around you. In some cases, that level of awareness is reduced if the events do not register as important and do not justify conscious awareness.

In addition, you become aware of thoughts and emotions moving into consciousness from the emotional memory system. Even in this case, however, you are conscious of these thoughts and feelings as happening NOW. As you read this, for example, you are aware of the computer screen or page, the colour of the type, the feel of the paper or computer mouse or touch of the ebook reader. As I make you aware of it, you will now become aware of the pressure of the seat against you or the feel of your feet against the floor. You will become aware of the colour and feel of your clothes. You may even become aware of the smell of your clothes or the air around you. Looking up, you will become aware of the colour of the room or location in which you are now reading. And shortly you will become aware of a difference in your breathing as you begin to understand you awareness of NOW, moment by moment. Prior to me mentioning these things, were you aware of them consciously?

If you become aware of a memory from the past, you become aware of it NOW. If that memory brings an emotion or other physical reaction with it, you do not become aware of it in the past. You become aware of it NOW. Whatever you focus your attention on can only be in consciousness if it presents itself in this very moment in time.

For your conscious mind, there is no past and no future except in memories and images. The past and future are the sole realms of your unconscious mind. However, your unconscious mind only works with the permission of your conscious mind. Your behaviours, emotions, and thoughts, while originating in the unconscious, can only take effect as a result of thoughts held in conscious awareness.

The conscious mind is the controller. Unfortunately, most of us allow the programming of the unconscious mind take control, thus abdicating our power and the responsibility for our lives. We simply become a slave to the thoughts and feelings emanating from our unconscious memory.

It is difficult for most of us to create a concept of such an entity as the conscious mind. It apparently has no form, yet it has supreme power over what we create in life. It can determine how we react to our environment and how we feel. As you will find through this program, it can even control the flow of information from your unconscious memory system and the emotional energy we store in it. To make our understanding of it a little more solid, we give it form by believing that it represents us as individuals such that we *see* it as being our shape and form.

At this point in the program, I won't go too deeply into my personal belief of what the conscious mind is—I will do that in Chapter 8. Suffice it to say that your conscious mind is the conductor; your unconscious mind is the orchestra.

YOUR UNCONSCIOUS MIND: THE GATEWAY TO THE PAST

Think of a library. Rows upon rows of bookshelves are filled with books of all sizes and colours. Each one is different from the next and is based on the experience of its creator. Each is a collection of pictures and words that record the memories and thoughts of an individual.

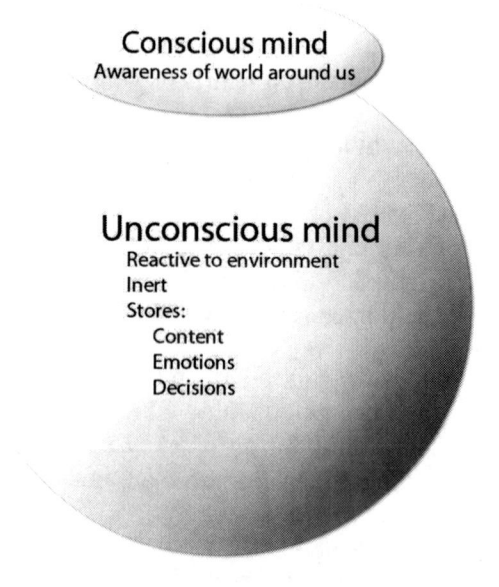

Conscious mind
Awareness of world around us

Unconscious mind
Reactive to environment
Inert
Stores:
    Content
    Emotions
    Decisions

Figure 1. A simple representation of the conscious and unconscious mind

The librarian knows where each book is and has a cross-referencing system that provides an idea of each book's content. The books are placed in order, with books featuring information on the same subject grouped together on the same shelf.

As with any library, many books address the same subject by are written by different authors. Each author has his or her own view on the subject, and there are likely to be totally opposite viewpoints expressed. (No doubt the book you are reading right now will be totally opposite to the beliefs of many!)

Despite this wonderful level of organisation, none of these books is able to change its content by itself. Even the librarian does not have the facility to change the content of the writings. So it is with your unconscious mind.

It records the events it experiences; and not just the events, but the circumstances that surround the events and the emotions and decisions made based on those events. Unfortunately, it does not always record information accurately. The information is sometimes not even true, but your unconscious mind records anyway, unable to change the incoming information or the behaviours that are produced as a result.

Where your unconscious mind records two totally different belief systems at different times, severe internal conflicts can occur. Your unconscious mind is not even aware that it has recorded conflicting views. It can only become aware of the internal turmoil that its reactive memory creates in consciousness.

With our library, the only way to change the content of a book is for someone to actively take a book down from the shelf, cross out or remove pages, and replace them with new information. Or, they can remove the book completely and replace it with a different version.

With your unconscious mind, the only way to change its recorded content is for you to take an ACTIVE part in bringing up an awareness of a memory, emotion, or behaviour and either modifying it or destroying it and replacing it with another. As you will see in this book's exercises, the awareness of a memory does not necessarily have to be visual. And, you need not bring up traumatic emotional experiences and relive them. It is sufficient to learn the strategies your mind is using to create your behaviours and emotions and using your conscious mind to change them.

YOUR MEMORY'S EMOTIONAL TIME BOMB

Even before you were born, your memory was recording. At that time, it was probably recording only the physical awareness, sounds, and vibrations of the world around you. You recorded your mother's emotions as she experienced the pregnancy, both positive and negative. You recorded your birth experience. You recorded the reactions of the people who surrounded you in your first few days of life in this body.

You have been recording your entire life. And, just like the library, your unconscious mind has been storing those memories in an ordered fashion, each memory given a coding based on similarities and emotions. Memories with similar emotions are stored together. Memories with similar colours, or shapes, or smells, or actions are coded so they can be found easily and accessed in the future in the same way the hard drive on a computer encodes information and stores it for retrieval when a program runs.

William James, the father of psychology as a science, described the formation of memory groups as being like pearls, strung together by the emotional coding of each memory. We call the first memory in these strings of memories the Original Root Cause memory. Memories with similar emotions or content are attached to each other in a similar fashion to a string of pearls, with the glue that holds them together being the encoding specific to their memory type of emotional content. For example, all memories relating to relationships with an encoded state of harmony will tend to be joined within that specific group. A simple knowledge-based group that relates to what a potato peeler is will comprise all memories you have of seeing, touching, or hearing about potato peelers.

Your unconscious mind has literally tens of thousands of these memory groups being added to every day through interactions with our environment, the people around us, and what we see and feel.

Why does it do this?

How Your Mind Really Works

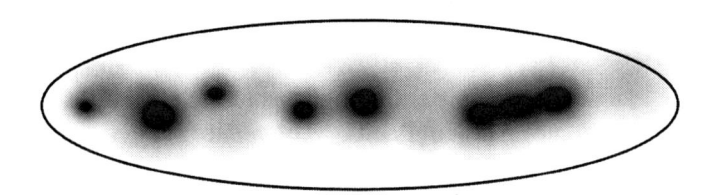

Figure 2. Memories joined and grouped together by their encoded content

The whole process takes place so that your mind can protect you. By having such experiences recorded, it can use the learning of these experiences to keep you from repeating negative behaviours or keeping you out of danger. Unfortunately, because of the way humankind has evolved and has been programmed, this protective mechanism often causes more grief than protection.

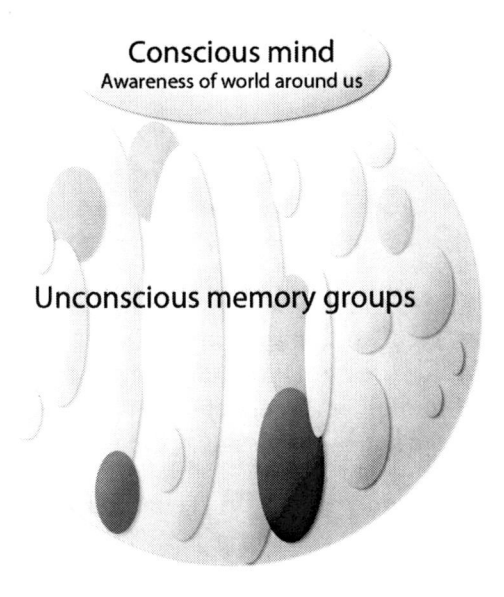

Figure 3. Memory groups within the unconscious mind

Such groupings of memories may never create any kind of negative influence and may remain unnoticed for the duration of your life. However, if the memory group has a large number of memories with the same emotion, or fewer memories with more intense emotional content, just one additional memory—called an Emotional Threshold Experience

(ETE)—can "overload" the system. Like the straw that broke the camel's back, an ETE often creates physical symptoms, conscious emotional trauma, and persistent thought patterns. Dr. Paul Goodwin, a neural physicist at Alaska Pacific University suggested that the emotional content of memory groups traps the emotion in physical change and has the potential to create blocks in the flow of energy and impede the flow of information through neural pathways. This can create anxiety and physical symptoms.

Symptoms may develop very suddenly in consciousness and show themselves as an apparent nervous breakdown. They may produce obsessive thought patterns or phobias. They often appear as disease states of varying levels of seriousness.

For example, Dr. Reike Hamer, a cancer specialist in Germany, noticed that he developed testicular cancer after his son was killed in a shooting accident. His curiosity stimulated, he began research in more than 10,000 cancer patients and found that, in every case, there was an ETE in relatively recent memory. A death, a marital separation, sexual rejection, fear or anger—all could contribute to the later development of the disease state. He suggested the trauma caused something akin to a minor stroke in a certain location in the brain, which later created a disease state in a particular part of the body. Each type of ETE caused its own brand of cancer.

Similar scenarios seem to apply to most disease states. Consider the division of the word disease. DIS-EASE: not at ease. This has always denoted a state of turmoil or discomfort. There are few states of turmoil more damaging to the human species than a mind in turmoil.

The bright side of the story is that Dr. Hamer found that by removing or dealing with the emotional content in the ETE, the cancer subsided or disappeared completely! Our experience has shown the same results, provided the Original Root Cause event is also addressed. Modern Neuro-Dynamic Strategies make this process far quicker than the more traditional psychological processes that Dr. Hamer used.

> **Dr. Hamer's Research: A Summary**
>
> After studying thousands of cancer patients Dr. Reike Hamer found that specific cancers are related to certain trauma:
>
> | | |
> |---|---|
> | Bladder | Conflict in marking your territory |
> | Bone | Loss of self-esteem |
> | Bronchial | Territorial conflicts |
> | Cervical | Refusing intercourse, man to woman |
> | Kidney | Territorial conflict 6 to 9 months prior |
> | Left breast | Generational conflict, woman–child or child–parents |
> | Liver | Deep-seated anger, often with financial problems over long periods |
> | Lung | Fear of death (own or others) |
> | Lymph node | Undefined fears |
> | Prostate | Sexual conflict, sexual self-esteem (males), loss of relationship/conflict |
> | Right breast | Nest conflict, non-sexual |
> | Skin | Conflict—ugly, dirty, happens to you, difficult time washing it off |
> | Stomach | Deep-seated anger, often financial or other long-term problems |
> | Testicle | Conflict with a child |
> | Uterus | Sexual conflict or with a child |
>
> These results are based on research with Dr. Hammer's clients over many years. There may be other contributing factors such as diet. All Dr. Hamer is demonstrating is that the Original Root Cause memory and the resultant memory groups trigger the disease state. See "New German Medicine" http://www.newmedicine.ca/ to make up your own mind.

Personal experience has shown me that the real story may be more complex than this with other physical and nutritional factors being part of the scenario. In reality, research shows that an alkaline body and a correctly working immune system make the development of diseases such as cancer less likely. And yet, if you combine the modern tendency of an acidifying diet and poor immune function due to overusing antibiotics, with the traumatic lifestyle and high stress levels under which most of the human race now labours, the increased incidence of "Western" lifestyle diseases makes a great deal of sense. Am I saying that we can now cure cancer in all cases? No.

Am I saying we have the total solution to preventing or treating cancer and similar diseases? Of course I am not. There are many aspects to disease states such as cancer, including the desire to die. I am saying, however, that significant resources must be put into research into the role energetic memory plays in disease states. The results clients have achieved through Neuro-Dynamic strategies have far exceeded the average result rate of success, which can be attributed to suggestion.

"But," I hear you say, "you said that the mind records all this information to protect me. Giving me a disease isn't protecting me, is it?"

Consider this. Your unconscious mind does not have the capacity to modify its recorded information. It simply records everything quite literally and uses that information to try to create harmony. It knows that, as a tiny baby, you felt most in harmony when you were being fed, held, and loved. Because you had very little overall experience at the time, these good feelings became very important and very desirable. In times of anxiety, you would call out or cry to attract attention and relive these wonderful feelings, through touch, warmth, and other pleasures. Of course, this is not the case with many babies who do not get this attention, and sometimes this lack of attention can translate into withdrawal and other anxiety based disorders later in life.

Kids and adults are not as cute as babies and often don't get as much attention as they did when they were infants. When something traumatic happens, however, you need that love and warmth even more. So, your mind tries to find a way to provide it. It remembers that when mum or dad or grandma or even a friend of the family was ill, everyone gathered around to provide support, assistance, and love. Later, the part of the mind that has added those memories to those associated with feeling good inside, without the ability to interpret the outcome, produces a disease state to provide the desired attention.

And it usually works, doesn't it? That part of the mind has done its job faithfully, even if it kills you!

THE CRITICAL FIRST FIVE YEARS

During your first five years, you live in a state of "waking" hypnosis. You have very little or no ability to analyse the information you are absorbing from your environment. You are not able to determine if the information provided by your parents, teachers, and others that may play a dominant role in your life is true or false.

You observe, hear, smell, taste, and feel. During this time you record the impressions that pass through your sensory apparatus. You also record a vast amount of information from your environment that does not come into your limited conscious awareness. Background sounds, sights that are just out of your field of focus, the temperature, the feel of your clothes against your skin, a breeze gently vibrating your hair. These "subliminal" parcels of information are placed in the appropriate book and on the correct shelf in your mental library. Because of this, there is a real danger for kids sitting in front of a television or being online!

Your awareness of emotions becomes especially important during this time because the relative degree of importance relates to the sum of all your stored knowledge and your ability to rationalise the emotion. Later in life, when you have stored a large amount of information about the same subject and may have "diluted" the importance of an emotion, the overall effect of a new memory may not be significant. But if you are one year old and starting to become really active, exploring the fascinating world around you, your relative degree of experience is very limited. An apparently negative experience takes on a huge level of importance.

The same event may seem insignificant when viewed with an adult conscious mind. For example, imagine yourself, one year old, wanting to see what that shiny thing is on the coffee table. You drag yourself up the side of the table, straining to touch the vase, which looks so appealing and maybe fun! Suddenly, your tiny legs collapse under you as the table tilts under your weight. The vase, flowers and all, rocks for a moment before crashing to the tiled floor and shattering into a dozen pieces. The flowers and water in the vase cascade across the floor at the exact instant that mum walks in to see what you're up to! As though your mum is a different mother, you see her face change from the smile of a loving parent to one of rage. The high-pitched scream of admonition stops you dead in mid-crawl.

The fact is that you had no idea that the vase belonged to your great-great-grandmother and was a priceless heirloom. All it was to you was a shiny object with soft colourful things sitting on top. You couldn't even tell anyone what it was because you had no experience with it and no language to describe it. Furthermore, your mind did not have the capacity to work through this amazing drama and come to realise that, as a family heirloom over a hundred years old, that shiny thing was so valuable that it could have kept you in food and clothes for a dozen years.

Your mind records just one emotional reaction. "That object is MORE IMPORTANT THAN ME!"

Of course, an adult with vast reserves of learning knows that a vase is not more important than the cute one-year-old baby. But the damage is done. The emotion of rejection, of not being as valuable as an inanimate object, has been recorded. More incidents are sure to follow and join this one in the self-image volumes of your memory.

This society values material things and being "better" than the next person. Because of the way we tend to process this input, the vast majority of people have a well-developed poor self-image by the age of six or seven. In addition, we often take on the turmoil, arguments, and violence within family situations. Because we cannot rationalise effectively at this early age, we create an energetic memory with awareness that we are a part of such turmoil.

Conscious window to the world

Limited unconscious experience

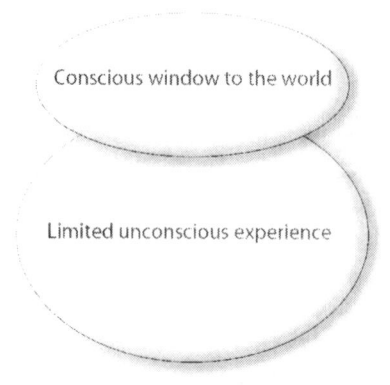

Figure 4. The limited experience of a five year old makes events larger in relative terms than does an adult

Very high levels of anxiety that develop in these years often present as serious problems later in life. When I first started this work, the average age of these disorders presenting was 20 to 30 years old. Now we see it at 15 years old and younger!

BELIEFS, VALUES, ATTITUDES, AND BEHAVIOUR

The mechanism of the mind is relatively simple. It is a process. The programming you take on follows through to a natural conclusion in controlling your behaviours and hence how you relate to other people. Even more critical to your future is how OTHERS respond to you, including family, workmates, and relationship partners.

Most of us tend to sabotage ourselves through our behaviours!

Have you ever met someone who you would have given your left arm to have them be attracted to you? You are on your best behaviour and do everything to impress. Just when you feel as if you are getting somewhere you do something so stupid you can't believe it was you doing it or saying those words. This amounts to self-sabotage. Let's explore why this happens.

As we have already seen, most of us are programmed with a poor self-image. Even if another part of us thinks we are okay, the original program is always there, ticking away in the background. As the emotional memory gestalts develop over time, the sum total of the memories and emotion form your belief systems. You develop beliefs about yourself, the people around you, your family, the weather, religion, sex, race, government, the best car to buy or drive, your favourite colours, and so on.

Every aspect of your being has a belief attached to it. Some beliefs have very little emotional content and just sit there in the background, not influencing you in any appreciable way. Others contain substantial emotional content that tends to surface in consciousness every time that belief is accessed with enough emotional kick to have an effect every time. Those that rate highly in level of importance to your unconscious protection system become your VALUES system.

Your values system, in turn, creates a series of priorities and determines how you feel about most areas of your life. Those priorities are seen by the outside world as your ATTITUDES and BEHAVIOURS. Every belief and value embedded in your unconscious memory is exposed to the world through the way you behave and what you say. What you do and say directs your relationships with every man and woman in your life.

Unless you learn to control your external behaviours by conscious intervention, your unconscious program is going to direct your life. It controls your level of happiness, your relationship disasters, your success or failure in business, and many other aspects of your life.

INTERNAL CONFLICTS

In clinical practice, I have found that 91% of clients with high stress levels or those who simply lack direction in life have two parts to their self-image. One part has been programmed to be relatively negative. A second part, having occasionally achieved positive outcomes, has recorded such achievements in another part of the mind. The information that each part supplies to consciousness as a result of a memory scan usually seems to be in conflict and thus elevates anxiety levels.

Other conflict mechanisms can revolve around future expectations, religion, sex, and a thousand other belief systems. Most never cause a serious problem, but when the energy level in two opposing memory groups is high, the results can, and usually are, catastrophic. Thirty per cent of the population in our society has internal conflicts of such intensity that severe biochemical imbalances are created. So that the body can cope with the resultant high adrenalin levels, it modifies its functions and changes its balance in nutrient requirements. Such imbalances have often been diagnosed as psychotic behaviour in the past and in the more serious cases have resulted in internment in a psychiatric institute. The symptoms of high anxiety levels and physical results are often treated with anti-depressants and tranquilisers such as Valium.

This whole process begins in the first five years of life.

If you suffer from high levels of anxiety, concentration or memory problems, dizziness or cloudy thinking, make sure you read Chapter 3 very carefully and implement its suggestions.

EMOTIONS AND BEHAVIOUR

The driving force behind your level of success or failure in life is the way you behave and the perception other people have of you. Your behaviour is controlled most of the time by the recordings in your unconscious mind.

Your basic beliefs are recorded during those critical first five to seven years. Over the next seven to eight years, you begin to think for yourself, and you are attracted to people and circumstances that fit in with these original beliefs. This is simply because your unconscious mind is trying to create an environment that is comfortable and harmonious. An environment and communication that is familiar in memory is sure to create what your mind understands is harmonious, even if the outcome may not be what you would consciously desire.

Maurice Massey, a sociologist, refers to this period as the modelling period. You tend to be attracted to people who have a similar "feel" and begin to become consciously aware of the things you value. As your unique values system is created, so too is your attitude toward life, people, and circumstances.

| **Socialisation Period 14 to 21 years** |
| Modelled behaviours tried in relationships with people outside the family |

| **Modelling Period 7 to 14 years** |
| Imprinted learning used to define role behaviours |

| **Imprinting Period 0 to 7 years** |
| Learning is taken on unconsciously |

The Massey Model of Human Development

As you have probably now learned, the only way you are ever aware of another person's attitude is through their behaviour. That behaviour includes the way they stand, the clothes they wear, their tone of voice, and the kind of language they use.

It is not difficult to see how the emotional content of memory groups affects your day-to-day behaviour and therefore how other people react to you. An underlying memory group associated with anger, for example, will produce behaviour that can be recognised easily as aggression. A memory group with high levels of fear related to self-image, on the other hand, will produce a person who is submissive or withdrawn.

By changing the way your mind processes information, it is possible to change the way you behave and consequently how other people perceive you and your values. Being able to change the strategies your mind is using also allows you to take control of your own emotions, behaviours, and future.

Consider what would have happened to your life if the behaviours and learning you took on during your Imprinting Period in your first five to seven years were all conducive to creating positive behaviours later in life. The Modelling Period would have provided you with a different set of external behaviours, consequently creating a more positive set of outcomes in relationships with others later in life.

By learning the strategies presented over the next few chapters you are going to develop a new and powerful relationship with your unconscious mind. The programming you take on during the unconscious Imprinting Period, and then the more conscious Modelling Period, is often negative and self-destructive. The Values built during these periods are the directors of the way you live your life, unless you change the programs you are running. Neuro-Com provides the tools to do just that.

FAST-TRACK LIFE ENHANCEMENT

That new relationship with your unconscious mind, one of cooperation and warmth, will empower you in a way you may have only dreamed of in the past. If you have carried long-term high levels of stress or trauma, you may believe it will take a long time to change the circumstances of your life. Certainly the old school will tell you that. **Don't buy that story!**

Your mind learns new strategies instantly when it understands that it is protecting you more effectively by providing the new strategies and behaviours. Remember when you learned that a hot stove or heater hurts when you touch it? How many times did you have to burn yourself before you learned not to do it? Most people learn in a microsecond not to put their hand where it is going to get hurt.

In the same way, your mind will take on new learning and behaviour instantly when you communicate to it that the new behaviour is better able to protect you than the old behaviour. When a part of your mind recognises an existing behaviour no longer conforms to creating protective mechanisms through the use of harmony, it will happily replace its old strategy with a new one, provided you supply it with one.

You are going to learn Neuro-Com, the language of communicating with your unconscious mind. This is a special language so powerful and so simple that you will be in total control of your own behaviour. In most cases, you will also be in control of the way other people behave toward you! The language YOUR unconscious mind uses to communicate with you at a conscious level is UNIQUE to you. No one else uses the identical system you do. For you to take control of this communication, you will engage in a new learning mechanisms that will give you a clear understanding of this process.

To do this, however, you must be thinking clearly, and you must understand why there may be some physical limitations to creating change that must be dealt with first. You will also come to appreciate why some of the people around you behave the way they do and that those behaviours will always affect your relationship with them.

The next chapter must not be skipped as it relates to the biochemical influence in communicating with your unconscious mind. If you have been under very high stress levels, this section will change your life. Your success in this life also depends on your communications with other people. With a clear understanding of why others may have behaviours you don't currently understand, you are able to more easily interpret situations in which you find yourself.

YOUR "SOUL"

We often hear the word "soul", usually in some religious or spiritual context. We hear about the idealised soul partnership or relationship where two people are so well matched they couple feel like one. But what is this "soul" we refer to so often.

Consider this: it is your unconscious memory that identifies you as being you. It is how it reacts to your environment that identifies that you are different from the people around you and even that you are different to objects around you. It is the programs running in the background in your unconscious memory that direct you behaviour, how you dress and how you communicate, the tone of your voice and the language you use. It is your unconscious memory that makes you YOU. You are the result of the thoughts, the feelings and emotions driven by unconscious programming.

We will explore the spiritual and relationship consequences of this idea in Chapter 8, but for now just keep this in mind as you progress through the various change exercises you will be exploring and you come to understand Neuro-Com.

Learning Journal: Consider your early life in terms of how you were raised, how your parents interacted and how they treated you. Consider your experience at school with both the teachers and other kids. Also, consider the role of religion in your upbringing, either directly or indirectly through the belief and values of your parents. In your Learning Journal write a list of all the learnings you may have taken on from others that now cause you grief in your emotional state or your relationships with others.

CHAPTER THREE

Possible Blocks to Your Progress

> **This chapter discusses:**
>
> - Biochemical blocks to progress
>
> - The role of psycho-nutrition in stress, self-image, depression and limiting behaviours
>
> - External influences: Being susceptible to the negative influences of other people and environments
>
> - Why others have so much power over you
>
> - The influence of religion in developing self-image

BIOCHEMICAL BLOCKS TO PROGRESS

Look around you at the people in your life. Take a look at society in general, and you will witness an interesting phenomenon. People in modern society are becoming very anxious, usually without knowing why. The levels of anger inherent in behaviour are becoming more pronounced, with incidents of violent or aggressive behaviour becoming more worrisome.

Over the past decade, the number of people who present themselves to psychotherapists, psychologists, and psychiatrists because they can no longer cope has increased dramatically. Sale of self-help stress management books and videos is increasing and the authorities are at last beginning to realise that aggression and stress have a significant role to play on the economy.

Most spend a vast amount of time and money trying to reduce their levels of anxiety, phobias, and guilt. Relatively few have succeeded by using "normal" treatments, and most end up on the never-ending cycle of tranquillizing drugs. The real problem is rarely addressed.

The tools you will learn in this program will allow you to change all but the severest of traumas at an emotional level. However, before you even begin to approach the emotional memory, we need to deal with some biochemical factors that create common physical stressors. Such physical stressors create a range of symptoms that are often misinterpreted as emotional symptoms and prevent your ability to assess the root cause of the problem.

In later chapters, you will become aware that it is becoming difficult to differentiate between mind and body. What affects one affects the other. The mechanisms of this interaction are complex; however, I will try to simplify the process so you can recognise some of the symptoms.

High anxiety levels are created in this society by the environment simply because we react to environment according to our internal programming. There are many sources of internal stress that continue to ferment below the surface, forever adding pressure to our personal emotional cooking pot. Common stressors include:

- Self-image conflicts
- Sexual self-image and belief systems
- Religious beliefs that fuel guilt
- Uncontrolled drives for success

Some people can cope with these; others can't. People react to the environment differently because each of us carries different memory systems based on the vastly different circumstances supplied by those in authority over us in those vital first five to seven years. A good example of wide variations in reactions due to environmental high stress levels is the Vietnam experience.

Some Vietnam veterans experienced the severe trauma of seeing and taking part in death and destruction on a vast scale, and yet returned home afterward relatively unscathed. Others found it very difficult to handle any unpleasantness at all and ended up under psychiatric care.

The greatest source of stress in most of us is the internal conflicts between different parts of our memory system. These internal conflicts can occur in a huge range of belief systems or memory groups when they are created at different times or under different circumstances. Perhaps the most powerful of these conflicts, which is very common in our society, is a self-image conflict.

As you have already learned, memories are processed in groups according to the emotional content of the memories or other "energetic" information encoded into them. Typically, you record a group of memories related to a negative or self-destructive self-image. In a materialistic society this is almost unavoidable as we are often trained to understand that "things" are more important than we are. We go to great lengths to protect the physical trappings of life but treat our own health and wellbeing with relative distain. Ninety-eight per cent of the human race has a deep-seated negative self-image.

On the other hand, most of us succeed at something during our lives, no matter how minor that success might be. Because the emotional or energetic content of the positive memory differs from that encoded in the negative group, such memories are stored in a separate memory group. As you create more successes, they are added to this new group to create a new belief system, but with encoding that is effectively opposite to the main self-image grouping.

When a new event in consciousness accesses the self-image belief systems, each belief system provides its automatic reaction to consciousness. You become aware of the positive, uplifting, aspect of your succeeding self at the same time as the negative, depressive self. Both reactions occur in your conscious perception at the same time and create an awareness of intense conflict or confusion. The rest of your mind interprets this as a serious conflict and produces physical changes appropriate to conflict by pouring adrenalin into the system. This process can produce dramatic results.

Belief and values conflict
Two opposite signals presented to conscious mind either at same time or alternating

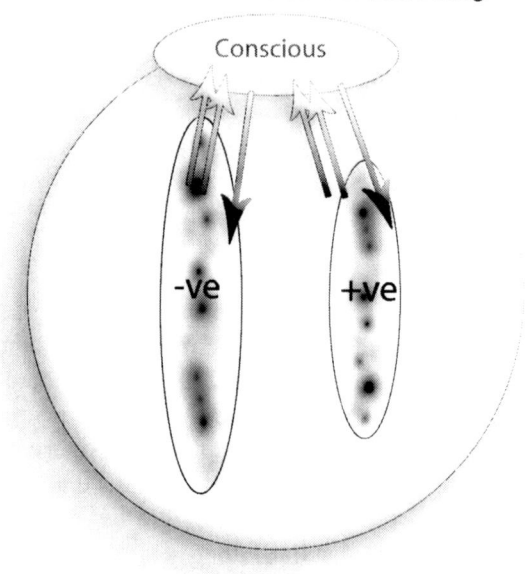

Figure 5. The origins of a self-image conflict

Adrenalin is a useful hormone when used as it is supposed to be used—to protect you. Its greatest value is to produce a physical change consistent with getting you out of trouble. This is known as the common "flight or fight" response. It is simply a way that your mind and body coordinate to protect you when you are in physical danger. In the good old days, when we lived in caves and wore loin cloths, we were subject to other predators using us as a food source!

Imagine, for example, that sabre-toothed tiger rounded a corner and surprised you as you went about your day-to-day survival activities. Instantly, your mind assesses the level of danger and begins to stimulate adrenalin release and other physical changes. Glucose is released into the blood stream, and you begin to breathe faster to take in more oxygen. The capillaries, small blood vessels in the skin and tissues, begin to constrict a little to control bleeding if you are attacked. Glucose and oxygen are transported to the muscles to provide extra energy for the muscles to react and allow you to run or fight as you have never fought before.

In this scenario, assuming you survived the attack, you would wander off and find a nice warm rock in the sun to relax again because the danger had passed. Your body would return to its resting state and a state of internal harmony. In the case of our internal self-image conflict, the elevated anxiety, driven by the flight or fight response, never goes away. Our self-image reactions are triggered a thousand times a day, continuously raising adrenalin levels. After a few years of this onslaught, the internal anxiety cycle becomes intense, and the body begins to respond in an attempt to restore balance.

The pancreas is stimulated to release more insulin to remove the excess glucose levels. Over a period of time it becomes extremely efficient in doing this. In fact it becomes so efficient it outstrips the level of glucose production and energy levels begin to drop. With long-term, high levels of anxiety these effects can take up to twenty years to really become dangerous. Typically, the victim becomes addicted to sweet foods or alcohol. Low energy levels are joined gradually by massive moods swings, often occurring within an hour of each other—happy after a sweet food fix, then depressed or anxious an hour later.

Other physiological changes also occur. It has now been found that high intake of processed grains, especially white flour, strips the body of essential B vitamins, which are needed in the energy cycle and in producing vital hormones and neurotransmitters.

Neurotransmitters are the chemical equivalent of a thought. They are a group of chemicals that are manufactured and stored primarily in nerve cells. They are used to transmit signals from one cell to the next. Different stimuli create different neurotransmitters. When the body is deficient in certain essential nutrients, these neurotransmitters cannot function properly. As a result, the nervous impulses that are critical for your nervous system to function correctly, do not work properly, and the nervous system begins to malfunction.

Poor nutrition can interfere with your nervous system in other ways. In their normal mode of functioning, nerve cells operate by transmitting electromagnetic impulses through the cell. This is done via an exchange of charged sodium and potassium ions in and out of the cell across the cell wall.

When an impulse reaches the end of one cell, the stimulus releases chemical neurotransmitters from reservoirs. These chemicals move across the tiny gap between cells (around one millionth of an inch wide) and are detected by receptor sites on the next cell. These receptors, in turn, stimulate the transmission of an impulse through that cell.

Both the transmission of the impulse and the transfer of the stimulus from one cell to the next rely on chemical processes. The availability of these chemicals relies on you providing your body with correct nutrition. Poor nutrition or an insufficient supply of essential nutrients causes your nervous system to malfunction. As a result, huge mood swings and perceptual problems can occur.

TYPICAL SYMPTOMS OF PSYCHO-NUTRITIONAL DEFICIENCY

Depending on the severity of the deficiency you or the people around you may experience some or all of the following symptoms. As you can see, some of them could be quite frightening if you don't understand their source!

- Concentration and short-term memory problems
- Sudden mood swings
- Inappropriate behaviour and emotions
- Uncontrollable tears
- Minor hallucinations such as the apparent movement of immovable objects
- Dizziness, feeling of the ground being soft or moving
- Hair trigger anger, sudden outbursts
- Paranoia, suspicion of other people for no reason
- Feeling of two or more individual personalities (this symptom is usually associated with severe energetic memory conflicts)
- Suicidal ideation
- Fear of impending insanity

Note that many of these symptoms have been associated with so-called mental illness. Most medical professionals have no idea what causes such symptoms and will deals with them at a superficial level or refer you to a psychiatrist or psychologist. My clinical files are full of cases of clients being told that they are hypochondriacs or need long-term psychiatric treatment or psychological counselling.

Certainly, a small percentage needs a support mechanism if they are suicidal while they are bringing the body back into biochemical balance. Even with clients who have run the gauntlet of counselling and a drug-induced stupor for years achieve startling results within two or three weeks by simply changing their diet and using nutritional supplements.

The thing that has amazed me continuously is that the bulk of psychiatrists and psychologists refuse to accept that foods affect thought processes and moods. Yet psychiatrists very quickly reach for mood-altering drugs. Unless I have missed some exceptional advances in food technology and drug technology, I swear that both consist of chemicals!

is that the drugs try (and often fail) to modify the
[prod]uced when the neurotransmitters in the brain are not
[as th]ey should. The nutritional approach, in contrast, modifies
[the pr]oblem that generates the symptoms first by fixing the
physiological issues that may interfere with nutrition processing or the uptake of food-based nutrients and then by ensuring the nervous system has an adequate, readily available supply to do the job.

Many factors interfere with our ability to provide our bodies with correct nutrition. Many would say that we can get correct nutrition from a good, balanced diet. This is absolutely true IF your body and specifically your gastrointestinal tract is functioning correctly. However, our Western diet is now loaded with a massive intake of sugars, dairy, and especially gluten-laden grains such as wheat, barley, rye, and oats. A very large part of the population is gluten intolerant, and the extreme end of that intolerance, Celiac Disease, is becoming a huge problem. Add to this a high level of tissue acidity and high sugar intake, and your body can no longer process foods or absorb nutrients correctly. Your gut becomes low functioning, you cannot rid your system of toxins and inflammatory diseases become the norm.

When these things happen, as they do more and more frequently, you are no longer able to supply your body with essential nutrients that are required for a whole range of functions, but especially the extremely sensitive nervous system. Consequently, we suffer from all the symptoms I have mentioned and even worse. We now believe that all the so-called mental illnesses are driven by such nutritional starvation, including obsessive–compulsive disorder, bipolar, and the entire spectrum of schizophrenias..

Important note: I am not diagnosing or trying to treat any medical or psychiatric problem here. If you are under the care of a medical professional, discuss the concept of Psycho-Nutrition with him or her. You may wish to refer them to some excellent works on the subject including:

Psycho-Nutrition by Dr. Carlton Fredericks

Nutrient Power by William J. Walsh PhD

The Schizophrenias, Ours to Conquer by Dr. Carl Pfeiffer

The Hypoglycemic Connection by Dr. George Samra

The Gluten Connection by Dr. Shari Lieberman

Alternatively, have your mental health practitioner refer to http://www.orthomolecular.org or to The Goulding Institute at http://www.thegouldinginstitute.com.

It is important to note that often the effects of such nutritional deficiencies are not obvious to many people. If you do not relate to the mood-altering effects presented here, remember that we often do not see such behaviour in ourselves. It is the way other people see us that has an effect on our personal relationships. From a personal point of view, begin watching your own behaviour in physical and emotional terms. Do you suffer from low energy on a regular basis? Do other people see you as nervous or irritable?

Often you will have to ask some trusted friends, who know you well, how they perceive your behaviour and moods. Listen carefully, and when several present you with the same perception beginning looking for an underlying cause if you don't like what they say. Ask yourself if your behaviour is likely to affect the way others react to you and whether this will affect your future. You may have to be very honest with yourself about this. And, if you don't have any friends to ask, you definitely have a problem with your future!

NUTRITIONAL SUGGESTIONS FOR EVERYONE

Clients and students often ask me, "Why can't I get all the nutrients I need from the foods I eat?" Because of our eating habits, food growing, storage and processing methods, and a host of other environmental factors, it has become almost impossible to get correct nutrition. If you could grow your own foods using well-nourished soils in an unpolluted, stress free environment, then eat those foods without over-processing or cooking them, you would get everything you need.

But you must understand that the pollution to which we are subjected, both atmospheric and the toxins we pour into our systems, destroy key elements of the nutritional cycle.

Internal toxins include things such as cigarette smoke, alcohol, sugars, drugs, caffeine, preservatives, insecticides, and so on. These toxins destroy the tiny finger-like projections, called villi, which line the intestines. Each of these villi, in turn, is covered by "micro-villi," even smaller filaments. There are roughly 20 million of these micro-villi per square inch. Can you imagine how small and fragile they are?

Normally, the cells that line the intestines are replaced every four to five days. Their function is to absorb the nutrients from the sludge that flows past and transport those nutrients, via the blood stream, to every part of the body. If the villi are not functioning properly, those essential nutrients are not absorbed and the rest of the body starves. Over a long period of time, the body begins to degenerate and induce disease states. Over a shorter period, such deficiencies will cause substantial mood swings as I have already discussed.

So, yes, you can get sufficient nutrients from your diet IF you are careful about avoiding the intake of toxic substances, remain unstressed, and select a balanced diet of unprocessed foods carefully. These foods should preferably be eaten raw to avoid heat degradation of the nutrients. Are you willing to do that?

DEADLY FOODS

Two foods are responsible for more deaths by suicide, stroke, and heart attack, than all the others combined. These two food groups are guaranteed to increase anxiety levels and cause psychotic symptoms. They are sugars and processed grains, especially white flour. And yes, they are the favourite foods of growing portions of our populations.

Advertisements say that sugar is natural. The inference is that it is thus okay to eat sugar in large quantities. The more you eat, the healthier you become. Most people only argue about its effect on your teeth. In 1915, we consumed less than one kilogram of sugar per person per year. Now we shovel almost 80 kilogram per year into a physical system that is not designed to process it.

In highly stressed people, the release of glucose from the storage mechanism in the liver is stimulated as a response to high adrenalin levels. The body responds by trying to take the higher glucose levels out of the system. It does this by stimulating the pancreas to balance the system. Because the pancreas is very efficient in its job, eventually the body is stripped of energy providing glucose. The system, starved of energy, responds by directing you to seek high sugar foods or alcohol. I have found that 85% of my clients are affected dramatically by such biochemical imbalances.

The symptoms I have described are typical under such circumstances. Adding the high intake of sugars to an already overloaded system makes the situation worse and further increases anxiety levels. Normal psychology or psychiatric techniques are useless under such circumstances, because thinking is seriously affected. Conscious communication is impaired.

When you eliminate sweet foods from your diet and increase protein intake, it does not take long to balance the system. Thinking clears and energy levels increase.

The other deadly foods are processed grains, especially white flour. During the early 1970s, a statistician was looking at figures related to admissions to mental institutions during the war. The fact that such admissions were halved during the war years had always mystified researchers until our number cruncher realised, by chance, that the availability of processed flour was reduced by the same percentage during the same period. This coincidence sparked a shift in the direction of research into mental disease, especially the schizophrenias.

Many aspects of psycho-nutrition are complex, and I have no intention of spending your precious hours describing them now. A complete explanation of the dietary requirements to eliminate the biochemical influence on your stress levels and ability to think clearly are included on the Neuro-Com web site at http://www.neuro-com.org.

Learning Journal: In light of what you have just read, use your Learning Journal to list the foods you eat and the chemicals you use each day that may have a toxic element. Evaluate your stress levels by scoring yourself for both anxiety and depression on a scale of 0-10 where 10 is the maximum intensity of these states. If either scale is over 4 out of 10 on average, you need to look carefully at dealing with the underlying biochemical issues. You can find more information on this at http://www.gmfint.com.

CHANGING OUR ENVIRONMENT

Being susceptible to the negative influences of others

Another major influence on the way we perceive our environment and ourselves is the way we interact with others and our perception of their role in our life.

How often have you decided to change your life and create something that is more nurturing for your future? How often have you craved positive attention from other people to give you a sense of value and purpose because you feel you are currently undervalued? How often have you come across a business concept that you believe can change your financial position and make life a little easier?

And, how often have the people around you cut you to pieces and destroyed your dreams through comments, remarks, and lectures about your ability? How often have you ALLOWED them to do this to you?

One area of greatest sadness for me in this life is the way people treat other people. We don't pay enough attention to how our words and actions might harm others, especially those closest to us. A careless word or the act of ignoring a plea for attention can have a devastating effect on someone else, and we are often not even aware we have done any damage.

In Chapter 1, I spoke of the global problem and the damage the human species has inflicted on itself. There is a simple solution to 90% of the world's problems that could be implemented easily through our schools and through parents being a little more concerned about the welfare of their children. That simple solution is the Principle of Edification. Implement this principle in your life, and your life will change for you and everyone around you.

THE PRINCIPLE OF EDIFICATION

We are destroyers. We destroy almost everything we touch. We destroy the natural resources of the planet and justify it as progress. We destroy our possessions and replace them without thought. We destroy the self-image of others around us by being critical of their behaviours and beliefs. And, we destroy nations and justify it in the name of our religious dogma.

I believe we do these things because it is a part of our own self-destructive mechanism. It is a less painful alternative to disliking who we are.

To make change, we must change. To like ourselves, we must like others. To like others, we must intervene in our current behaviours. Let me ask a point-blank question. Use this as a serious exercise in creating a new, unselfish future:

When did you last unselfishly complement your partner, a friend, or an associate on his or her looks, behaviour, or friendship qualities?

If you are in a position of influence in your job, when did you last tell one of your staff that they did a good job?

Gentlemen, when did you last take notice of your wife or girlfriend's new hair style or clothes and tell her how much you liked them?

Stop for a minute and think seriously about this—it is vitally important. Also search your memory for the last time someone complemented you on anything.

I know from both clinical and public experience that 99.9% of the human population never complement those around them or do it so rarely that it is difficult to remember.

It's very sad, because a small word of praise can change a life. This applies especially in that first critical five years when our mind is a sponge, seeking any word or behaviour that tells us we are valued. A touch, a hug, a kiss, a smile, a word—each is as powerful as the next in developing a strong positive self-image and teaching the same behaviour to our children. Do you remember a moment in your life when you did something or created something or won a game of skill and received genuine praise or a word of encouragement? Do you remember how you felt in that moment?

If you learn and implement this one important lesson in this life, then your value to the survival of the human race has just been enhanced a thousand fold.

The Principle of Edification simply refers to the power of building someone else up through a word of praise or a supportive action. You can make a huge difference just by looking for the good in other people and offering a word of praise. Initially, it may be a little embarrassing if you have never done it, but get accustomed to doing it. You will get your reward by watching the look on others' faces. Some will get such a shock that they won't know how to react externally. But, I guarantee you will make a lifelong friend.

The majority of humans are so focussed on themselves that to spend time making other people feel good is as foreign as walking on water. We are so quick to criticise and so fast to resort to anger as a means of expression that most of us are always on the defensive. Those who express aggression and anger drive the rest of us into a shell, too fearful to do the things we would like to do because we don't want to be criticised.

I have seen this behaviour a thousand times in individuals who have a poor belief in themselves. They create avoidance behaviours that limit their potential, just so they won't be criticised by their peers for trying to be different or upgrade their situation. Small business is a great example. I'm sure you have known people who would have loved to start a business and change their financial situation. But, they give up under the cries of derision from their friends and family.

What sort of insane behaviour is that? What would happen if we turned that attitude around and made it a source of praise to encourage individuals to expand their horizons and do better for themselves and their immediate family? What would YOU do if just suggesting in conversation that you wanted to be financially independent brought a kind word from your friends rather than laughter?

Can you imagine what would happen if our teachers all started enhancing our children's self-image by praising the things they do? By teaching self-value, our children will learn a different way to deal with each other and consequently with strangers. By creating a consistent educational environment and transferring that into the home, we could create a new form of the human race within a couple of generations.

I call this self-involved behaviour the I-Virus. It is a disease that is all pervasive and has infected most of the human race. Like any other virus, it replicates itself and mutates to fill any gap it can find. It destroys its host, just as the global I-Virus is destroying our earthly host. This virus will be our undoing if we don't take a stand—if you don't take a stand and do what YOU can to support the people around you.

The Principle of Edification is powerful. By adopting it as part of your personal philosophy, you will find your world will change for the better. People will want to be in your company because they feel good just for having spent time with you. You will find you will do more business just because people want to deal with you. Your relationships will be more solid because your partner will feel safer with you. By putting out such energy, you will draw it back to you a hundred fold.

Exercise: The Principle of Edification

A wonderful exercise Skip Ross, author of *Say Yes to Your Potential*, used to teach will give you a fulfilling challenge that will set precedence for you when we begin to discuss Neuro-Com strategies.

For the next 24 hours make the firm commitment never to criticize any person, place, or event in your life!

Get your family involved and have them remind you if you slip up. Why is such accountability needed? Because there is a second part of this exercise that makes it work:

If you do slip and are critical of anything, the 24 hours starts again.

By the time you have completed a 24-hour period according to this exercise, your life will be more fulfilling and peaceful.

A Summary of the Principle of Edification:

Always look for the good in people and situations. Even if they are nasty pieces of work, there is always something that is good. Remember that behaviour is driven by past programming and is not necessarily under their control.

Offer a word of praise to those around you, even if it is a minor compliment on the way they look, act, or talk. Make your comments genuine and believe them. You will be discovered if you are not sincere.

What's in it for you? You will feel better about your own self-worth in the scheme of things. You will find you have friends you would never have imagined, and people will clamber to do business with you. Isn't that enough?

Learning Journal: Spend some time thinking about your life and the people around you. How many people actually provide you with praise and support. How many people do you know do you spend time with because they make you feel good about you? What is it that they do that makes this so? Now think about how the people around you would feel if you applied the Principle of Edification to them, and you made them feel valued and loved. Make some notes on this principle and how you can change your behaviour to make people want to be with you.

THE PRINCIPLE OF VACUUM

This is another principle of life I learned from Skip Ross many years ago.

You have no doubt seen a movie of a space adventure or an aircraft scene where the hull of the craft was punctured, and everything is sucked toward the hole and out into space. While such scenes may be frightening (especially for the poor individual that gets sucked through a 6-inch square opening!) such a scene makes for a great lesson: the Principle of Vacuum. Air moves rapidly from an area of high pressure to an area of low pressure. Wherever there is a vacuum, air and anything in that air will be sucked toward it.

The same principle seems to work in life. I indicate "seems" because it has been my experience with hundreds of people that this principle operates consistently. Put simply:

Dispose of what you don't want to make room for the things or events that you do want.

By removing the physical items around you that you no longer want or that no longer fulfil a purpose, their energy to be replaced by the things, events, or people that you want in your life. This principle also applies to people, but I suggest you be a little more cautious of exercising this principle in this regard, especially family!

Here's how it works. Your unconscious mind creates energetic attachments to everything in your life. Everything you accumulate as part of your world is energetically installed in your memory's filing system for future reference to be retrieved as and when necessary. The problem is that unless you consciously expend effort to provide other instructions to change the energy content of that memory, your unconscious mind continues to place a level of importance to those items, events, or people.

Over the years this accumulation can become burdensome and begin to affect the way you perform by limiting your ability to create new situations. You are emotionally bound to a past that may not be conducive to making the changes you want. Before we start to move in the direction of programming a new NeuroPrint (life plan) for you, you need to give your unconscious mind some basic instructions on what is important to you now. For example, I will give you an illustration that may ring some bells for you immediately.

Let's say you are an entrepreneur. You enjoy creating businesses and would love to savour the benefits of wealth and lifestyle that accompany this pursuit. You have tried starting many businesses, but find that for some reason, something has been missing in the formula. You just could not find a way to create the outcome you desire. Part of the reason could have been the lack of support from family or friends; it could have been a fear of talking to other people; it could be a lack of belief in the product or the people involved in the business. The flavour attached to these past enterprises is lack of success. (I use "lack of success," because we tend to avoid the idea that we failed!)

Over the years you have accumulated lots of paperwork, business tools, products, videos, and tapes of all of these business ventures. Being a well-organised soul, you have put all this information neatly in a filing cabinet or in a box or under the bed. You now want to get on with a new venture that will create your fortune.

Your conscious mind is willing. This is because part of your mind knows and believes it is possible for you to succeed, despite what your family and friends say. Furthermore, you regularly meet people who are doing it and who are creating a new lifestyle from their efforts.

Your unconscious mind, however, is sitting there with its emotional memory watching every conscious thought for instructions on what information you want it to present to you. As you know, it does this to ensure you have all the information and resources available to fulfil its highest intent for you, to protect it and create harmony. So, your unconscious mind sees you are getting into a new business and responds by processing all it has on new business and presenting it to you in the forms of what it considers valid information and behaviours.

It accesses everything. It not only processes the memories of your inherent ability to achieve your goals, but it also has full information about the past lack of success. Of course, that lack of success must be real, and it must be valued because you still have all the paperwork from those past business ventures, for example, carefully stored away. If you still have such artefacts, it must have value to you. Thus, a valid response is to implement behaviours you have used in the past, even if they recreate the failure.

Remember, your unconscious memory has no ability to rationalise the information it has stored. It merely presents it to consciousness for validation and action. Neither can it differentiate between what is real, and what is vividly imagined.

Remember the Principle of Vacuum—get rid of what you don't want so that you can make room for the things, events, or people that you do want in your life. In the example above, what do think you should do? Just eliminate everything from your life that does not support your desired outcome or that you have no intention of ever using again. In this example, it is the paperwork (provided you are not legally required to keep it for tax purposes), the videos, tapes, products, order forms, and so on.

Other aspects of your life are the same. Anything you store that has no positive effect on the future you desire should be removed from your life. Your mind still uses energy to keep those memories in place. This may apply to clothes in your wardrobe, tools in the shed, paperwork, books, magazines, jewellery, old electrical equipment, and so on. It encompasses anything you don't use or will probably never use again. One good assessment of value to you is if you have not used it in the past 12 months, chances are that you will never use it. If there is a negative emotional energy attached to an item, get rid of it regardless of whether you use it or not.

Check through the list of people in your life. Who supports you? Who criticises you? Who do you find provides good energy to your relationship? Who leaves you drained when they have gone? Make a list and check it twice. Find a way to distance yourself from those who drain your energy or who do not support your endeavours for the mutual good. You cannot afford to engage with people who drain your energy or provide negative feedback when your intent is to create a different future.

Remember the definition of insanity:

"To continue doing the same things you have always done, in the same way you have always done them, and expect the outcome to be different."

Learning Journal: Think about the people and things in your life that occupy your time and energy. Do they contribute to your values? Do they make a real positive difference to your life, either because of what you do for them, or what they do for you? Spend some time thinking about this and write your thoughts on how your life would change if you did not spend time and energy on people and things that don't really matter.

Exercise: The Principle of Vacuum

On the following pages you will find Principle of Vacuum Stocktake List, one for Physical Possessions and one for People. Print as many copies as you require or use your Learning Journal

Spend some quiet time filling in each form according to the instructions, making sure you include everything and everyone in your life. Walk around your house and office while you make the possessions list so you don't forget anything.

Then, pack up anything you have not used for the past 12 months and either sell it or give it to a charity. Get rid of it! Anything that has severe negative emotional connections, destroy it! If it feels good to do so, have a ceremonial burning or smashing session.

For people who drain your energy, find a way to stay away from them. If necessary, explain to them why you are doing so. The knowledge of their effect on people may help them change their life also!

I know that this exercise will be difficult to complete for many. But it works and is often enough to bring amazing new events, people, and things into your life quickly. It gives a clear instruction to your unconscious memory to delete the emotional charge connected to the past.

Principle of Vacuum Possessions List	
Item	Location

Principle of Vacuum People List			
Name	Emotional Effect on Me	Distance myself?	How?

CHAPTER FOUR

Communicating with Your Mind

> **This chapter discusses:**
>
> - Neuro-Com: The language your conscious mind uses to communicate with your unconscious memory
>
> - How to accurately assess your mind's unique communication methods
>
> - Thought: Feeling reactions, disturbing the flow
>
> - Making friends with your mind
>
> - Conflict resolution: Parts integration
>
> - A power example: Removing your worst phobia in five minutes!

NEURO-COM

> **Important: You are about to learn one of the most powerful mind-changing principles ever understood. Make sure you make plenty of notes regarding how your mind relates to this information and complete all exercises.**

Neuro-Com is understanding the methods your unconscious mind uses to communicate with you at a conscious level and with the unconscious programs of other people around you.

Most methods of personal development and mind control suggest that you talk to yourself or repeat affirmations a million times to convince yourself that you can really create the things or circumstances you want.

In reality, this method works for very few simply because very few unconscious memory systems use verbal communication with any level of authority. Language is simply an interpretive medium in communications. The real power in communicating with your unconscious mind is in the pictures and feeling reactions that come to consciousness for acknowledgment and instruction. Let's look at the process your mind uses in general terms and then look at the exact process YOUR mind uses for you.

SIGHT, TOUCH, SMELL, TASTE, AND SOUND

The next 20 minutes may be the most important in your life because you are going to understand clearly how your unconscious mind is controlling every thought and emotional reaction you have and how you normally react to them.

Let's take some time to look at how your mind handles a positive program so you can see the structure of YOUR internal communication. Remember, the method your unconscious mind uses to communicate with you is essentially unique to you. Your past programming is different from anyone else's, because you have lived in a different environment, had a different education and had different people around you. As such, it is essential to recognise and become comfortable with your own communication patterns.

Exercise: Your Positive Program

Take a minute of quiet reflection and think about a significant **positive** emotional memory from the last five to ten years. Don't try to analyse the content or the circumstances surrounding the memory. Just be aware of the memory itself. It may be a birthday, a holiday, a romantic moment, or a childhood memory. As you conjure the memory, relax into and become fully aware of it. We are not going to get into the events leading up to the memory or the consequences of that moment, just the memory itself.

What is your perception of this event? How does it present itself to you? What do you see internally? What do you feel? What do you hear? If you process memory visually, you may see an image in the back of your mind or even as a picture postcard in front of your face. As you become aware of your event's memory start to look at it from the perspective of HOW your mind is presenting it:

- Determine if it is clear or foggy.
- Is it a still image or a movie?
- Is it colourful or black and white? Does a specific colour predominate?
- Is it light, medium, or dark?
- Does the image appear as though you are in the middle of it, surrounding you, or does it appear as a postcard out in front of you?

As you become aware of it jot down a few notes in your Learning Journal. We will do this is more depth as we progress and as you understand more about the process. For now, just write details of HOW that memory is presenting itself, not the content.

As you look at the image, or even if you are not aware of the internal image, begin to become aware of the *feelings* that are embedded in the memory.

There may be emotions in the memory.

How do you feel the emotion? What emotion are you aware of? Which part of your body do you feel it in, around the heart, the stomach, your back, tension in the head? In other words, what physical sensations make you aware that this emotion is what it is?

Are you aware of any sense of vibration or temperature change in any part of your body? Does the memory feel warm, neutral, or cold?

Do you get any sense of touch with the memory? If you were to "touch," the memory, would it feel smooth, rough, soft, or hard?

By now you may be getting an awareness of what we are trying to do. You see, apart from some memory links that are based on content, your mind uses certain strategies of visual and emotional processes to represent the energetic content of a memory. As you progress through these exercises, you will see that specific types of memories use exactly the same formula. That is, the visual characteristics are the same and the kinaesthetic (feeling) characteristics are the same. Although it is less common, most people have some awareness of sound, smell, or taste in the memory as well with its own characteristics.

For example, a particular individual may find that positive memories tend to be colourful, vibrant, three-dimensional movies where the person is actively "inside" the memory. The image may be sharp with a slight yellowish tint. The awareness may also be warm and peaceful with a playful background sound.

The same person when accessing a bad memory may find that it may present as just a few frames of a movie playing over and over again. The images may be dark and foreboding with a general feel of coldness. The emotion may be fear, which is felt as a tightening of the stomach muscles and edginess in the legs and arms. There may be a high-pitched sound pervading the scene.

In each case, good or bad, that same person accessing another memory considered to be good or bad would tend to process all such memories with the same qualities. All bad memories tend to be dark and foreboding for this person. The mind's strategy for labelling is generally the same in every case. This is because each of us learns in a specific way. Some of us learn visually, some learning by feeling and touch. If you have any doubts about this, try remembering a smell from your childhood, like the smell of freshly baked hot bread. See what memories come back and how vivid they are!

An excellent example of this is the way people process a phobia.

Exercise: Removal of a Phobia

Warning: If you have a phobia that creates intense fear and that is uncontrollable do not proceed with this exercise alone. Certainly, you should read through the information contained here. Just by doing that, your unconscious may realise it is not really protecting you and may drop the behaviour. Try to understand the method your mind used to create the behaviour and how it can use other, more suitable strategies to protect you. You will understand how your mind communicates with you.

A phobia is simply a part of the mind that has encoded a group of memories in a way that creates extreme fear and avoidance behaviour. It does so as part of its highest intent for you, that is, protection. Such intense fear is often created by non-logical input and is related to several events coupled with moderate emotional content, or a single highly emotion-charged event that is coupled in memory with life-threatening danger.

I have helped hundreds of people overcome lifelong phobias in minutes just by showing them the strategy their mind is using to create the fear, then "doing a deal" with that part of the mind to use other, more appropriate strategies. For example, let's take a look at a common phobia, the fear of spiders. Just the idea of looking at this one may be making the hairs on the back of your neck stand up, but please come with me on this. If you have such a phobia you may find it is gone at the end of this exercise.

Before we begin, it is important for you to understand something clearly. Right at this time, your unconscious mind is aware of what we are discussing, and if it is creating phobic behaviour in you then we know it is doing it for one reason only: protection. Part of your mind is using the specific strategies of the phobia because, based on what it has been told, it believes that your response to its strategy will keep you away from the consequences of the causal event. And, because it is trying to protect you in the only way that it knows how, we cannot really lay blame for the terrible feeling that the phobia generates. However, we can give it some new, more powerful and more appropriate responses with which it can protect you. That's fair enough, is it not?

The Neuro-Com Program

Please note: If you have a phobia of a different nature, the same process applies as we discuss this particular event. Simply see how you process your fear.

Okay, back to the phobia itself. Fear of spiders is probably the most common phobia because we come across them so frequently. I have dealt with hundreds of arachnophobias. The mind's strategy is almost always the same. The person's unconscious mind creates intense fear using a visual strategy of presenting an internal image of a massive, hairy black spider within striking distance of the person's face or on an arm or leg. Often, the awareness is of multiple venomous eyes staring at the victim. (How am I doing so far? Sound familiar?)

The body responds by pouring adrenaline into the system in a typical "flight or fight" response. In most cases, the desire to run becomes paramount, and the victim gets well out of the room or environment that contains the spider that triggered the event, even if the spider was a tiny money spider on the other side of the room. Usually the phobic's mind does not differentiate and will create the same response just with *the idea* of a spider close by. Big black hairy spider; that just has to be dangerous.

What your unconscious mind does not realize is that while some spiders are dangerous, most are not. Yes, you do need to be careful of them. But in most cases, if you just steer clear of them whenever possible, the level of danger to you is virtually zero. So rather than protecting you, your unconscious mind is actually putting you in danger by raising anxiety levels to an abnormally high level, certainly beyond what is necessary for a nonlife-threatening event. It can use better strategies, more appropriate to the circumstances, if it is provided with a better way to respond. I know that part of your mind is aware of this, so we are going to give it permission to access the rest of your unconscious mind for some better strategies to use as we discuss this.

Let's give your mind a new instruction. You used to be good at creating the phobic reaction; therefore, when you do this correctly, you will be able to test the result immediately to know your mind is doing the right thing by you. Most phobics can create the response just by thinking about the source of the phobia. Do it now, but keep reading.

First, forget about any emotional reaction that arises. It is of no consequence here, just your awareness of the event. See and feel what the mind is presenting to you. If it is fear of a spider, become aware of what the presenting image is and look at the colours involved. Are they dark and cold, or do they have other characteristics? Do you see eyes that look dangerous or are you aware of the texture of the image? You may still be aware of a level of anxiety, but that's okay for a second or so longer. Now I ask you, as your unconscious mind is watching, change an element of the image and awareness of the trigger memory. If it is a hairy black spider, ask your unconscious mind *"What colour it would be if it were friendly and harmless?"*. You will probably find the image will change immediately. Give the face of the spider an idiotic grin like the Cheshire Cat and notice that the anxiety is fading or has gone or is different in some way. We have given your mind permission to get new resources to protect you in future so that it no longer needs the old strategy of inappropriate fear.

In this process, you have taken an old strategy that your unconscious mind has presented to consciousness and deliberately changed some aspects of that response. Rather than going along with the automatic thought/feeling reaction to which you were accustomed, you have provided your unconscious mind with a new response to use—a new instruction. By communicating with it in a way it understands, it will accept the new program and implement it whenever it is asked.

You are in control of your reactions to thoughts and feeling reactions presented to your conscious mind.

YOUR PERSONAL NEURO-COM

I chose a phobia to use as an example because it is often the most dramatic way to produce an amazing result for you quickly. If you can take a phobia out in a few minutes using these strategies, imagine what you can do with the rest of your life!

We are now going to take a close look at the Neuro-Com strategies YOUR mind uses so you can learn its "language". Once you understand this, you can create anything you want, free of the restrictions your mind may have placed on you in the past. It is as though you can suddenly talk

The Neuro-Com Program

to someone who speaks only in an Arabic tongue and clearly understand them.

How your mind handles emotions

First, we will go through a series of exercises using different memory types to determine how your mind processes information with different emotional content. Over the next six or so pages you will find a series of forms headed with the prime human emotions:

Love	Guilt
Hate	Envy
Anger	Desire

There is also a copy with no heading that you can print off and use for any other aspect of your life you wish to work on in future. On the left of each page you will find a list of visual, kinaesthetic, and auditory characteristics that your mind may use to create your awareness of each emotion. Read the instructions in the following exercise carefully, and then use the forms to complete the exercise.

Exercise: Learning your Personal Neuro-Com Strategies

Make some time when you can sit comfortably alone where you will not be disturbed for half an hour. Get a book to support the forms and a pen or pencil so you won't have to break your concentration. Become aware of the existence of your unconscious memory system. If you wish, give it a kind of personality that provides you a feeling of warmth and friendship and that allows you to feel as if you are both working toward the same goals. Become aware of how it presents itself to you. You may even be aware of more than one part of it; that's okay. I'll explain why you may have this awareness in the next module.

Now we begin. Start with the form titled "Love." If love does not give you a positive feeling, then start with one of the others that does. (It is unfortunate, but some people have never allowed love into their lives so may not be able to get a clear awareness of it. Most do however.)

Now allow yourself to relax into the images and feelings related to the emotion. See any pictures or videos that may come up. Be aware of any internal feelings that may present to you. Try not to dwell on the events that are happening in the memory more than is necessary to bring up the awareness, but become aware of the characteristics of the images and feelings as they present.

Work down the page in front of you and become aware of each of the characteristics in turn. How do they apply to your videos and images and feelings and sounds as they represent the emotion with which you are working? Make notes on each characteristic that applies. If a particular characteristic does not apply to this emotion, just leave the comment space blank. If there is something you become aware of that is not listed, make a note of it separately. Everyone processes memories differently.

Neuro-Com Characteristics Checklist

For: The Emotion of Love

Visual

Self in or out of picture	
Framed or panoramic view	
Bright or dull	
Black and white or colour	
Three dimensional or flat	
Sharply focussed or blurred	
Movie or still image	
Number of pictures (if stills)	
Intensity of colour	

Feelings

Warm, cool, or cold	
Texture: Rough or smooth	
Vibration: Mild or intense	
Intensity of feeling	
Size	
Shape	
Weight	
Movement	
Steady or intermittent	
Internal or external	
Pressure	

Auditory

Volume	
Pitch	
Direction	
Tone	
Rhythm	

Smell
Taste

Neuro-Com Characteristics Checklist

For: The Emotion of Hate

Visual

Self in or out of picture	
Framed or panoramic view	
Bright or dull	
Black and we white or colour	
Three dimensional or flat	
Sharply focussed or blurred	
Movie or still image	
Number of pictures (if stills)	
Intensity of colour	

Feelings

Warm, cool, or cold	
Texture: Rough or smooth	
Vibration: Wild or intense	
Intensity of feeling	
Size	
Shape	
Weight	
Movement	
Steady or intermittent	
Internal or external	
Pressure	

Auditory

Volume	
Pitch	
Direction	
Tone	
Rhythm	

Smell

Taste

The Neuro-Com Program

Neuro-Com Characteristics Checklist

For: The Emotion of Envy

Visual

Self in or out of picture	
Framed or panoramic view	
Bright or dull	
Black and white or colour	
Three dimensional or flat	
Sharply focussed or blurred	
Movie or still image	
Number of pictures (if stills)	
Intensity of colour	

Feelings

Warm, cool, or cold	
Texture: Rough or smooth	
Vibration: Mild or intense	
Intensity of feeling	
Size	
Shape	
Weight	
Movement	
Steady or intermittent	
Internal or external	
Pressure	

Auditory

Volume	
Pitch	
Direction	
Tone	
Rhythm	

Smell

Taste

Neuro-Com Characteristics Checklist

For: The Emotion of Anger

Visual

Self in or out of picture	
Framed or panoramic view	
Bright or dull	
Black and white or colour	
Three dimensional or flat	
Sharply focussed or blurred	
Movie or still image	
Number of pictures (if stills)	
Intensity of colour	

Feelings

Warm, cool, or cold	
Texture: Rough or smooth	
Vibration, Mild or intense	
Intensity of feeling	
Size	
Shape	
Weight	
Movement	
Steady or intermittent	
Internal or external	
Pressure	

Auditory

Volume	
Pitch	
Direction	
Tone	
Rhythm	

Smell

Taste

Neuro-Com Characteristics Checklist

For: The Emotion of Desire

Visual

Self in or out of picture	
Framed or panoramic view	
Bright or dull	
Black and white or dolour	
Three dimensional or flat	
Sharply focussed or blurred	
Movie or still image	
Number of pictures (if stills)	
Intensity of colour	

Feelings

Warm, cool, or cold	
Texture. Rough or smooth	
Vibration: Mild or intense	
Intensity of feeling	
Size	
Shape	
Weight	
Movement	
Steady or intermittent	
Internal or external	
Pressure	

Auditory

Volume	
Pitch	
Direction	
Tone	
Rhythm	

Smell

Taste

Neuro-Com Characteristics Checklist

For: The Emotion of Guilt

Visual

Self in or out of picture	
Framed or panoramic view	
Bright or dull	
Black and white or colour	
Three dimensional or flat	
Sharply focussed or blurred	
Movie or still image	
Number of pictures (if stills)	
Intensity of colour	

Feelings

Warm, cool, or cold	
Texture. Rough or smooth	
Vibration, Mild or intense	
Intensity of feeling	
Size	
Shape	
Weight	
Movement	
Steady or intermittent	
Internal or external	
Pressure	

Auditory

Volume	
Pitch	
Direction	
Tone	
Rhythm	

Smell
Taste

YOUR STRATEGIES EXERCISE REVISITED

Now that you have spent time looking at how your mind processes information, you should be starting to see some patterns emerging.

There are three basic scenarios that you may find as a result of this exercise:

All emotions accessed use exactly the same visual and kinaesthetic clues to represent an emotion, with perhaps some minor variations in the location of your body's physical responses.

Each emotion may be presented through totally different strategies with clear definition between them.

The positive and negative groups of emotions each demonstrate similarities. For example, negative emotions such as anger and guilt may be processed the same way, whereas love and desire may be processed similarly.

As you undertake these exercises, you may begin to understand why it is necessary to treat each individual as different and that change mechanisms are unique for each person. However, as you begin to see that the change mechanisms are purely a step-by-step process, you will clearly understand that you can control all aspects of your life relatively simply. All we are doing here is defining how YOUR mind functions and communicates for you.

MAKING FRIENDS WITH YOUR UNCONSCIOUS MIND

Many people believe that because of the apparent negative outcomes their mind seems to create, their unconscious mind is the enemy. Let's face it, for most of us, life does not progress smoothly, and we don't live in the utopia that our dreams indicate we deserve. As such, we blame the people in our life, or we blame our unconscious mind for attempting to trip us up. Given these tendencies, I am going to repeat something that is important for you to take on and accept.

Your unconscious mind is not trying to prevent you from doing anything. It does not try to make you unhappy, and it never lets you down. **It never does anything that it has not been told to do.**

Your unconscious memory system is just that—unconscious. It seems unaware of its own existence apart from producing automatic responses to the immediate circumstances surrounding it. It responds automatically according to a program that it has been provided with in memory and cannot vary that program unless YOU intercept its responses and provide it with new information.

I'd like to repeat the explanation of how it works: you become aware of something or an event through your senses, consciously or just below the level of conscious awareness. Your unconscious mind takes in this sensory awareness, evaluates it for similar past events recorded in memory, and responds by presenting visual, kinaesthetic, or behavioural strategies that conform to its belief system regarding the appropriate behaviour under similar circumstances. I know this was longwinded but it's a simple system. Your unconscious mind only responds with behaviour that it "knows" has worked before. It is a *reactive* system.

If you want to start communicating with your memory, does it not make sense to make friends with it? Think about that. If you treat your mind as an enemy, the perception it receives is that it should behave as an enemy. It can't tell that you don't really mean something you tell it in a particular context—it can only react. It will scan its memory system for information on behaviours that are the correct way to treat an enemy. What emotional and behavioural mechanisms do think it will give you? Do you really want to go to war with your mind? I think not. It makes a great deal more sense to make friends with your unconscious mind with the intention of having its responses provide you with the support and comfort afforded through friendship.

Now that you have seen a glimpse of the way you mind processes information for you, how do go about making friends with your mind? You could talk to it, but our mental institutions are filled with people who talk to imaginary people. Let's give that one a miss in case someone hears you.

Take a look at the strategy your mind uses for the emotion of Love. How does that emotion present itself? The following is an example only and you should use your own strategies as we work through the example. The following is a summary of how a mind might work to represent love:

EXAMPLE AWARENESS

Individual: Teenage girl

Image: A dog, small, long-haired, white

Visual strategies: Image is a movie, intense colour with a shift toward yellows, slightly blurred, three dimensional, individual is "in the movie."

Kinaesthetic strategies: The feel is generally soft and warm, like touching a kitten. There is a feeling of movement with an awareness of a soft ball in the chest just below the heart. The "ball" seems to change in size, and it exerts a steady, internal pressure toward the front of the chest.

Auditory strategies: A low, muffled hum with no specific source. It rises and falls slowly.

As you see, we are less concerned with the actual event happening in this awareness than with the characteristics that are presented. This is the Neuro-Com for this particular young girl when dealing with a positive emotion of love. Later in life, the image may change to include boys, but the basic characteristics of the presenting image will usually be the same. However, as you will see, if later awareness of the experience of love becomes negative, say with an adult relationship with a partner, the presenting characteristics of love may change. Interestingly though the change will only be relevant to the type of love connected to the adult relationship. The characteristics of love when related to a dog would not change unless she had a traumatic experience with dogs.

Now we'll take a look at how this girl could create a congruent friendship with her unconscious mind. First, we need to create a perception of a friendly mind. For most, it is easy to give the image or awareness a human character but that is not essential. Here we could start with something that might stimulate an intelligent dialogue, for example, a wise old man with a long beard. This represents a mind that can provide us with immense learning from the millions of books stored in his mental library.

Feel free to make it a woman, an animal, or a god-like creature if you wish. To create a spirit of loving cooperation between them, we are going to modify the awareness to create a feeling of love.

We take the basic picture of an old man and turn it into a three dimensional movie that seems just slightly blurred. We give it a slightly yellowish tint as though in sunlight and then move into the movie to become part of it (associate with it). We are now in a warm, soft environment where we can communicate telepathically with our wise unconscious mind.

To complete the friendship, while having the wise old man in our presence, we add the feeling of the soft ball in our chest, with a slight outward pressure. We mentally acknowledge this being as our unconscious mind with a loving relationship with him. The creation of this awareness is now consistent with the representation our teenage girl

---

Exercise: Making friends with your unconscious mind

Use the example provided to create a friendship with your own unconscious mind. Make sure you work through the characteristics provided in your evaluation of the emotion of love or another appropriate positive emotion.

In most cases, you will find that the image or awareness (it may not be a visual awareness) will come to you easily because just the idea of creating it will give your unconscious mind instructions to provide suitable concepts. If it does and it feels right, go with it.

Take your time and become comfortable with the process.

had of love. By creating this image and moving into it, she will now be able to communicate with her unconscious mind with a strong element of friendship. He will work with her to create the outcomes she wants.

TAKING CONTROL

If you have worked through the examples and exercises in this chapter, you should now have a clear idea of how your mind processes information. If it is not clear yet, go back and repeat this chapter before moving on.

After that, if you are still not sure, you may wish to log on to the website to see if any queries you have are in the Frequently Asked Questions (FAQ) section. Many of the most common questions are answered there. If you are still having problems, go to the "Contact Us" page and fill out the form. I will respond to you as soon as possible so you can achieve the best results from this chapter before you move on.

Website: **www.neuro-com.org**

With your understanding of basic Neuro-Com, we can turn to the practical aspects of using this knowledge to create change. Over the next three chapters, you will learn how to remove undesirable emotions, handle conflicts, and develop a new future through designing your new NeuroPrint. Then, we will look at how Neuro-Com works within relationships, and some of the critical aspects of belief and values systems when dealing with other people in your life.

CHAPTER FIVE

Practical Neuro-Com

> **This chapter discusses:**
>
> - Stacking the deck in your favour
> - Neutralising negative emotional responses
> - Removing negative family links
> - Removing the anger
> - Dissolving guilt forever
> - Self-image: Removing the conflict
> - Removing destructive parts conflicts
> - Your values system

STACKING THE DECK IN YOUR FAVOUR

The degree of success we create in our lives depends on how other people respond to our personality and behaviour. As you read in the previous chapter, your unconscious program creates your attitudes, which in turn creates your external behaviours. Everyone you come across in life observes your external behaviours and these behaviours determine how they react to you.

Think about the people in your life to whom you are attracted and with whom like to spend time. Think as well about the people with whom you repeatedly do business and the characteristics they present that make you feel you can trust them and make you comfortable.

There are several ways your mind processes such information and provides responses that may or may not be appropriate to the outcome you wish to create.

You observe other people at two levels:

- Conscious
- Unconscious

CONSCIOUS OBSERVATION

The conscious level of observation we use is usually inaccurate unless we have trained ourselves to observe. What we see, hear, feel, and smell in any environment is always coloured by our unconscious memory system so that we are often aware of something that is different from reality. I remember in my younger days reading Sherlock Holmes stories and being amazed at the deductions the master detective made based on accurate observation and study. Very few of us have such abilities, preferring to accept generalisations in our contact with the external world. With such low demands on accuracy, we see and hear what our unconscious mind presents to us rather than reality.

An example of this is often quoted in law. If a room full of people all witness the exact same crime or event, everyone will provide a different version of the event. This occurs because each individual has a different set of memories relating to that incident type and environment and will provide different emotional, visual, acoustic, and kinaesthetic responses. What you think you see is not always reality, but merely reality as your unconscious mind perceives it.

UNCONSCIOUS OBSERVATION

While you are busy with your thoughts and actions at this very moment, your unconscious mind is taking in a thousand times more information than your conscious awareness. Consciously, you are only able to process the information you are concentrating on in the moment we call now. This may be sensory input from eyes, ears, touch, taste, and smell, or it may be the thoughts on which you are concentrating. However, your senses actually pick up new information in your environment at a much greater rate. What is not impinging in consciousness is processed by your unconscious mind.

The thousands of subliminal (below the conscious awareness) signals are sorted and stored in the memory ready to be accessed when they are needed. If the unconscious determines that some of those signals deserve your immediate attention, you will be directed to that source of signal instantly. Again, this is a protective mechanism, but it allows you to know a great deal about situations and people you come across without really knowing why you know it. Your unconscious mind is aware of such subtle distinctions as change in skin colour, dilation of the pupil of someone's eye, the way they walk, distant sounds, and odours of which you're not consciously aware. All these signals are used to determine if a situation is comfortable or dangerous or if you should like or mistrust the person with whom you are dealing. A lot of so-called intuition is derived from these sources.

Just as you detect tiny details of other people and assess them on that basis, they also assess you on your behaviours. As we have discussed, these behaviours are derived from learned responses based on beliefs, values, and attitudes. Anything that affects these micro-behaviours tends to affect the way people treat you and interact with you. So, if you are stressed or carry negative emotional content in your memory, it can and does change the way others react to you.

It is very useful, therefore, to remove as many of the negative influences in your life as possible to maximize the usefulness and enjoyment of your relationships with other people. This, in turn, will affect your level of success in life. Anxiety and anger have the greatest influence in this regard.

Expectations society places on you and the demands you place on yourself create substantial levels of anxiety for most of us. Expectations or demands of family and friends can influence how you process information and what you observe of the world around you. And, your reaction to different groups of people based on unconscious reactions influences how others respond to you. It is therefore important to know how to remove undesirable reactions and programs that influence behaviour or anxiety levels. This section covers the effects of these anxieties on your body and emotional system, and how to eliminate a substantial component. Why is this important?

Think about the people you like to be around. Do you like to spend time with people who are anxious and jumpy, or do you prefer people who appear in control, calm? Most of us would answer the second question affirmatively because such people tend to lend stability to the rush of modern life. They appear to know what they are doing and even create an air of knowing something about life that you may not.

The physical and emotional components of stress and anxiety have a serious effect on thinking processes and your perception of the world around you. They can cloud your thinking, create sudden mood swings and muddy the waters when it comes to dealing with other people. Because your success in life usually depends on the perception other people have of you, it is obviously important that you remove such apparent negative effects.

This entire chapter addresses eliminating conflicts, creating very subtle levels of rapport with people in your life and making them want the things that you have or know. It is also about having you think clearly so that your unconscious mind has a clear image and feel for other people and circumstances.

To do that, we need to get something out of the way first. We need to make sure you are giving yourself the best chance in the world to use this information efficiently. We need to ensure that all sources of stress and anxiety are understood and that any physical components can be removed. Your mind can then concentrate on the task at hand.

NEUTRALISING NEGATIVE EMOTIONAL RESPONSES

A major influence in your life and behaviours is your family and the people you deal with daily. Personal history is often crowded with relationships with other people that have not turned out how you would like. In an ideal world, one would be close to all family members and would feel comfortable with everyone you deal with in business. Alas, such is not often the case.

If you spend a few minutes reflecting on your life, you may be able to identify some of your dealings with other people that contain high levels of anxiety. This is common in strained relationships with family or former friends, business associates, or even organizations such as companies or churches. The anxiety or anger still held in these memories will always affect you in a damaging way and will influence your decisions when you meet people who either look or act the same.

The Neuro-Com strategies we are about to work through will provide you with a method for removing inappropriate anxiety and anger.

Removing negative emotional links

When you reviewed your life, how many relationships with individuals or organizations produced a feeling of anxiety or anger? When you explore these emotions, it is common to get the feeling that there is some kind of "link" between yourself and the entity that created the emotion.

As an example, think of a relationship that contains a significant amount of anxiety. If you can't find one in memory, congratulations; I bow before you in humility! I still suggest you work through this exercise just to get an idea of the Neuro-Com process. Most people do not access the full details of the event or person, but produce a vague image or kinaesthetic awareness that does not feel nice. It will typically produce feelings of heaviness, darkness, or a darker colour such as red or grey; an awareness of a "foreign" body of some sort within your chest or stomach and sometimes inside your head. Some people feel as if the "presence" is outside them, but very close by.

Take your time and determine the characteristics of the event or relationship you are thinking about. It's a good idea to print off a fresh copy of the Neuro-Com Characteristics Checklist you used in the last chapter (www.neuro-com.org/downloads) when you assessed the major emotions, and use this to work through this exercise thoroughly. Trust the responses you get; they are coming directly from your friendly unconscious mind, at your request.

Now read through the following process carefully so you understand the steps clearly. You may need to close your eyes as you actually work through it for yourself.

NEURODYNAMIC DETACHMENT

Removing Anxiety or Anger

The NeuroDynamic Detachment method is simply a way of accessing your unconscious memory and providing it with a new instruction; that is, telling it that the former behaviour of creating anxiety or anger is no longer appropriate. At the same time, you will negotiate a more appropriate unconscious response.

You can do this with eyes open or closed. I suggest, however, that if your eyes are open, stare at a particular point and let your eyes defocus so you are not taking in any clear visual signals. Most people find semi-closed or lightly closed eyelids work best, without strain.

Exercise: Emotional detachment

Read through the entire exercise before you begin so you have a complete understanding of the process. You don't want to stop half-way through to check details of the method!

Step 1.

Allow yourself to float up and out of your body, way up in the air so that you have a perception of being able to look down on the world. Take your awareness off the external world and become aware of your new floating environment. Whatever you mind perceives is okay for you.

Step 2.

Become aware of the individual, organization, or event that causes you the anxiety or anger. Feel the emotion by being aware of the characteristics of the presentation, as we have practised. If your mind presents the emotion as being inside your chest, perhaps a solid ball with a specific colour, make a mental note of how it presents itself to you. Take your time and get accustomed to the feeling and visual clues.

Step 3.

Use whatever means is comfortable for you to move away from your awareness of the entity or event. If it was inside you, move it outside and away. As you do this, it is highly likely that you will be aware of some kind of connecting cord between it and you. It may be a thread of light, a rope, or a solid rod. Whatever your mind projects is okay. All this means is that your mind has not yet been given permission or an instruction to let it go.

Step 4.

Begin to move away from the entity. As you do, you may or may not get a clearer visual idea of it or the person involved, but your perception of the connecting cord may become clearer. Bring the image or awareness of your friendly unconscious mind, as you created in the last chapter, into this field of awareness and have him/her/it stand next to the cord.

Step 5.

It is important for your unconscious mind to understand that although the injustice that may have been done to you may not have been fair at the time, continuing to attach the negative emotion to the memory no longer serves a protective purpose. In fact, it is now doing more harm than good. Anger or frustration always cause physical harm over time and has been proven to shorten life expectancy.

Ask your mind to store the learning from the event so it can be used in the future if appropriate, but having done that, it would be okay to let go of the negative emotional content of the memory or relationship, would it not?

You will be aware of an internal positive response or acceptance of this premise. Ask the mind to cut the cord or use any method it wishes to dissolve the connection with the event or individual. Watch what it does, and you will probably be aware of a change in the look or feel of your perception of the person or event immediately.

Step 6.

Thank your mind for fulfilling its highest intent by protecting you better, and then allow the scene to dissolve and float back down into your body. Open your eyes.

The Neuro-Com Program

If you have developed a good relationship with your unconscious mind during previous exercises, and processed this exercise correctly, you will now be unable to access the old emotional content of the memory. In fact, you may find that the harder you try, the less emotional or the funnier the memory becomes. Neuro-Com Detachment is a powerful ally. It is a direct device that your mind understands because you are communicating an instruction in language it understands. With a little practice, you will find your unconscious mind is way ahead of you and will delete negative emotional responses from memory before you can even go through the process. The more you consciously practice Neuro-Com strategies the more your unconscious mind makes it a part of its immense repertoire and takes just a single conscious thought from you as an instruction to run the whole program instantly.

As previously discussed, your unconscious mind will not (cannot) continue to employ a strategy that it newly understands is causing you harm. It learns instantly and will drop the old behaviour as soon as it comes to the understanding that continuing the behaviour will cause you further harm. The old idea that it takes months or years to make change is false when using Neuro-Com strategies, because the intervention is using "language" that your unconscious mind understands and responds to. It's "language" is that of visual images, feelings, tastes, sounds and smells – not of words that do not easily convert to simple positive images.

The Spaceship Strategy

By now you should understand how to create understandable communication with your mind so you can understand the next process and how it works. It is another form of detachment that may appeal to a scientific mind.

The first steps are the same. Float up above your body. Become aware of the event, individual, or organization that creates the negative emotion within you. Bring the entity outside your body and bring your unconscious mind into the scene as before.

Now, create an awareness of a spaceship nearby. Give it some detail so that its design and purpose are clear. With your unconscious mind having stored the learning from the event for future use, load the image or awareness of the event or individual onto the spaceship and launch it into space, along with the old, inappropriate emotional contact. Thank your mind and float back down to your body.

This is a very simple exercise, but is very effective in the results it achieves.

Dissolving guilt forever

Guilt is the most useless emotion the human race ever created or inflicted upon itself. It serves no purpose other than to increase anxiety levels and provide people in positions of power with even more power at our expense.

The origins of guilt come from the religions. I don't mean that they come from the core of the religions but from the controlling dogma with which humans have managed to surround the religion. Guilt is a simple emotion based on one of two premises:

1. We do something that someone to whom we have given power says we should not do, or
2. We don't do something that someone to whom we have given power says we should be doing.

The most common causes of us carrying guilt revolve around religious or social laws involving sex or money.

While the modern world claims to be mature in its handling of sexual matters and discussions, reality tells us differently. Most people have sexual hang-ups based on religious and social taboos put in place hundreds of years ago. We often claim comfort with the idea of our sexuality, but in an open discussion with our peers we clam up and avoid the discussion except in joking terms. Men have difficulty talking to women and visa-versa. We often feel sexually inadequate because of the way the media and glossy magazines surround it with in terms of expectations. And even when homosexual and lesbian relationships are openly accepted as part of society, many heterosexuals treat such matters with disdain or discomfort.

Millions of people suffer deep guilt and anxiety over sexual beliefs or ideas they have that fall outside what they have been taught in their early years is acceptable. Just like a self-image conflict, we create two different sets of memory groups around sexual issues. One is the set we received as children: that sex is something to be kept behind closed doors and that the only acceptable sexual encounter is heterosexual. This belief system is driven essentially by the religions. The other sexual memory grouping is formed as we are exposed to the world and find that almost anything goes according to the magazines and news.

We are then in a position that if we follow the second memory group, our unconscious mind presents guilt as a response to the earlier, much more deeply embedded belief system. If we follow the earlier system, we feel inadequate because we don't feel comfortable with the modern expectations or acceptance of sexual encounters. Either way it's difficult to win!

Money also creates conflict with many people. You may be surprised at the number of people who carry guilt because they have been successful financially or who sabotage their own success because they have a deep-seated belief that anyone who makes a lot of money must be a crook. The guilt surrounding this issue is just as illogical as the guilt surround sex. In both cases, it's almost as though we tend to feel guilty because we have something to enjoy.

I have no intention of discussing religions and the rights and wrongs inflicted on us by them. You are free to believe what you want, when you want, and how you want. Furthermore, I suggest you be the only one who has any input into that decision. You alone should decide what is right or wrong based on the standards you wish to set for yourself. Rob Roy McGregor is quoted as saying:

"Honour is the gift Man gives to Himself"

How true! We are responsible for our own behaviour toward ourselves and toward others. Once we have selected a standard of behaviour that suits our beliefs, or changed our programming to accept our behaviour, what purpose is there to guilt if we harm no one?

I have tried to avoid expounding upon my beliefs in this program because it is all about YOU taking responsibility for YOUR own internal communication and teaching you the tools to be able to do it. But please indulge me for a moment. I believe that unless the human race removes the controlling influence of the powerbrokers within the religions that claim the authority to interpret what is right and what is wrong, the human race is doomed. I say this after having studied religions and metaphysics in depth for more than 50 years.

Those in authority have taken the simple core truths of an omniscient intelligence of which we are all part and to which we are all connected and used their own pathetic interpretations to collect power and money from the masses. They have started wars and inflicted guilt and suffering on millions. They have tried, at times, to manipulate banking and the world economy. Their priests have taught one idea while living an opposing life themselves. And yet we still give away our personal power to them and take on the guilt they inflict on us.

If you want to remove guilt from your life, you will need to look at your belief systems in depth when it comes to the base programming you have received at home, in the churches, and at school. If you harm no one in your daily activities, who has the right to judge you? And, if you learn to love yourself, why judge yourself and create pain and anxiety for yourself?

I do not apologise for the irritation I display toward the churches. I have chosen not to remove that anger from my system because it drives me to finding a better way to help people lead a fulfilling life, free of guilt and anxiety that serve no purpose. Like many others, I have spent a lifetime seeking a useable perception of reality that does not revolve around other individual's beliefs. To that end, I have started a global, no-rules organization that studies the NeuroDynamic Principles in relation to spiritual fulfilment through Cheyzen. There will be no room for guilt or control of any kind, just understanding, acceptance, and unconditional love (www.cheyzen.org)

How do we remove guilt when it is often so deeply embedded throughout our psyche? For many, it will simply be a process of using a NeuroDynamic Detachment process that we have already discussed and practised. The same principles apply to assessing the guilt perception and the characteristics of the emotion and simply changing the perception with the help of your unconscious mind. This works for most people. So, if you carry guilt, take yourself through this reframing process.

If you have a strong religious background, you may need to do some thinking about your basic beliefs. This will almost certainly involve looking at some of the conflicts within that belief system and probably self-image conflicts. Before you do anything, however, make sure you have a clear understanding of the next process I will take you through.

SELF-IMAGE: REMOVING THE CONFLICT

Have you ever felt that there seem to be two or more parts of you, often in an eternal battle for supremacy? A surprising number of people do. It usually doesn't cause a problem, just a minor irritation at times that causes confusion or odd behaviour. A growing number of people, however, have a bigger problem with this phenomenon and the problem needs to be addressed.

Sometimes these "parts" conflicts present as a level of minor confusion as to what action to take. Decisions are difficult to make because one part of you makes you feel as if you are okay and you can do whatever you need to do, while at the same time another memory group is saying you can't because you are too stupid, don't have the skills, or are just not good enough in some way. Sometimes, such conflicts present as an intense anxiety. Often they present as a lack of self-confidence in some circumstances, while you may feel great in others. You usually don't understand the inconsistency.

In Chapter 3 we covered some of the internal blocks to creating change in our lives. The chapter included a section on psycho-nutrition and the effect of disturbances in the neurotransmitter function in relation to stress. People who suffer from causal high stress, and hence high adrenaline levels, often present with substantially more powerful self-image conflicts. About 7% of the human race do, or will at some time in their lives, hear voices. I am not talking about having an internal conversation with the self. I am talking about hearing voices that are not real, just as you would hear during any normal, face-to-face conversation. It is extremely disturbing for those who have this disorder, mainly because the voices are often angry, critical, abusive, or threatening.

Such voices are usually someone who the voice hearer knows. Often many different voices talk at the same time. Years of clinical experience with such disorders has shown two causes that always act together.

A History of self-image conflict and emotional trauma during early life

One cause is psycho-nutritional deficiencies, which disturb the flow of signals from thought to the brain and hence the neural pathways responsible for hearing, and in some cases, seeing.

Second, anxiety, guilt, and anger are almost always underlying emotions in such issues at the extremes of the scale. But self-image conflicts can still cause all sorts of problems at the lower end of the scale as well.

A self-image conflict is created when two separate root cause memories are stored in memory with opposite emotional content but with similar informational content. Your self-image groupings begin forming from birth. Each time self-image is called on from consciousness, we add further memories to the original, building a belief system about who we think we are and how we feel about ourselves.

Belief and values conflict
Two opposite signals presented to conscious mind either at same time or alternating

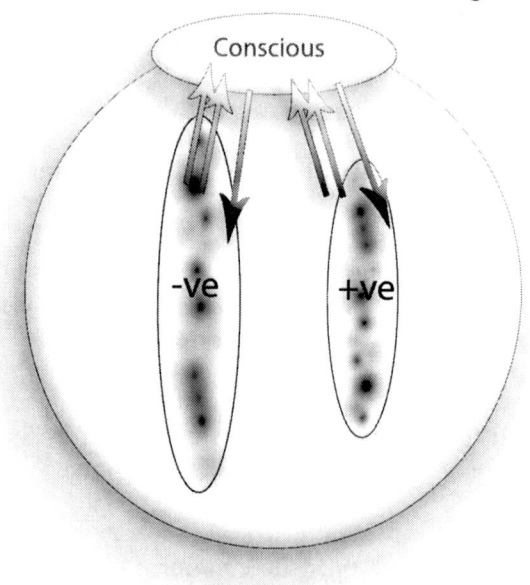

Figure 6. Origins of a self-image conflict

Because of the way our society operates, we usually receive mixed signals about our value to our environment. Some of these are discussed in Chapters 1 and 2 as we explored the development of memory and its emotional groupings.

There are many occasions where we are provided positive feedback from parents, teachers, and others in authority in that first vital five to seven years. There are perhaps far more instances when we are given some bad feelings about ourselves.

As the two memory groups develop, the amount of energy in each increases so that the conscious emotional responses get stronger and stronger. Eventually, the levels of conflict between the two presenting self-images begin to create an awareness of anxiety and self-doubt. As anxiety levels increase, we start pumping more and more adrenaline into our system. Over time, we begin to become aware of some of the physical results of long-term anxiety. We have discussed these in Chapter 3 so I won't repeat the symptoms. Suffice to say that the damage such self-image conflicts can do is horrific from the point of view of the individual who suffers them.

Most people are aware of some level of self-image conflict. Even when the emotional trauma is not great, we are aware that at least two parts of us exist because we are aware that one part of us feels okay about ourselves and another lacks confidence.

It is important to understand that the individual parts of your memory seem to have no awareness that the other exists. They just automatically react to conscious demands for information. The parts are not maliciously trying to disturb or confuse you. They just don't have any other strategy to use or instructions from you.

Now that you understand how to communicate with your unconscious mind, you will probably find a dozen variations on the exercise we will use here to remove this particular conflict. This process is:

- Asking your unconscious how it perceives the two or more parts with which it has been working.
- Confirming its intentions in doing what it has been doing
- Giving it new instructions to work differently.

In this exercise, we will assume there are two separate parts of your memory system that relate to your self-image. You will be aware of them through your normal day-to-day activity but may not have recognised that they have a form.

You will notice as you move through this exercise that you are becoming more aware of the components of your mind. As different parts present themselves to you, just accept that whatever is presented is how your mind perceives itself. In other words based on all the stored knowledge, thoughts, and emotions stored in the memory groups, the visual, kinaesthetic and auditory representation it provides you is your mind's perception of itself under the current circumstances. It may seem a little naïve, or even childish, in the way it presents itself. Don't be tempted to try to change it. Just go with it and enjoy the experience.

Read through this exercise in its entirety before proceeding, and make sure you understand the principles behind it before trying it yourself. No harm will come if you don't complete it in one session; it just won't have the desired effect. However by understanding the process and completing it the first time, the results are enhanced.

Exercise: Removing Self-image Conflicts

Sit in a relaxing chair in a warm room so you are comfortable. Place your hands face up on your knees a few inches apart so they are comfortable. Let your eyes close comfortably and begin to become aware of your friendly unconscious mind as we have done before. Be aware of its presence and that it is receptive to working with you.

Now become aware of the positive part of your self-image memory system and ask for it to present itself to you by taking some visual or kinesthetic form on your left hand. In other words imagine that your unconscious is presenting this part of your mind to you by bringing it out onto your hand. As you do you may be aware of an image of a person, an animal, or a shape—it could be anything. Whatever is presented is okay; accept it. Become aware of its characteristics in look or feel, shape, colour, and behaviour. Thank it for coming. It should now be placed comfortably on your left hand.

Now ask your unconscious to present the apparently negative self-image and have it come out onto your right hand. Again, become aware of its characteristics and thank it for presenting itself to you. Whatever it presents as is okay.

You should now be aware of the two parts, one on each hand. They will now be aware of each other and may express some surprise, perhaps a little irritation that the other exists, but this is okay. The rest of your unconscious is also there watching this. Now, communicating internally to the positive part, ask it what its highest intent for you is. With all its behaviours and resources what does it really want for you—what is its very highest intent? Whatever it answers or gives you an impression of, reply to its answer with another question "For what purpose?" In other words, we want to know why it is doing what it is doing. If you continue to do this it, it will eventually answer, "To create harmony," or "to protect you." Thank it for its answer.

Now turn to the so-called negative part and ask it the same thing. Go through the exact same process. Eventually you will find that it also will come to the same reply "to create harmony" or "to protect you"! What a surprise. Both parts of your self-image want the same thing, even though they have been using different mechanisms in the attempt to create it.

They will probably both be a little surprised by now and will become aware that they should be working together in some way. You now need to provide them with a means.

Communicate with both of them along the lines of:

"Because you both want to protect me and to create harmony for me, it would be okay for you to combine resources in some way and work together, would it not?" They will agree. Continue…

"Then it would also be okay for you to find a way to re-integrate, to come back together into one part, and be a thousand times more able to fulfil your highest intent for me? Please now find a way of combining to become one".

Now just sit quietly and watch. You will see them find a way to come together, combining into one integrated self-image to properly fulfil their highest intent. Often, a new image of a new entity, object, or representation will replace the original two entities. Whatever is presented to you or how this happens is okay. Don't get a fright or be surprised if your hands begin to move together without you wanting them to. It is common for your unconscious mind to create such behaviours. Just let them come together if they want to as the two parts join forces.

Be patient and allow them to come together in their own time and way. When the process is complete, the image and awareness of the single resultant part will be different and will look and feel very different to you. Typically it will feel as if it is more powerful and friendly. Bring it back inside you as the rest of your unconscious watches and integrates the new part into itself. Enjoy the feelings that may now move through you. When you are ready, come back into the room and open your eyes.

* * *

Please don't underestimate the power of what you have just done in this exercise.

You have gained the attention of your unconscious mind and two parts that have in the past, seemed in conflict. You have allowed each of these parts to present itself in a way that it perceives itself. You have created rapport with each part.

You have communicated with each in a way it can understand and respond and have made each aware of its true intent for you (which it may not have been completely clear on before). You have given it instructions to find new resources to use so that it can more ably and more efficiently protect you through creating emotional harmony.

Most important, you now understand how to take control over emotional behaviour and thoughts that you didn't know were in your control. It is not unusual for people who use this process to become aware of a real state of calm that persists after it is completed. New self-confidence and a new ability to create a different future are common. This exercise is an important component of the exercises we cover in "Designing Your Future" in the next chapter. Without such self-image conflicts, there is nothing to stop you from creating exactly the kind of future you would like.

OTHER MEMORY CONFLICTS

Self-image is not the only part of memory that can have multiple components. Because of the world we live in and the many sources of so-called authoritative learning, we tend to create several sources of internal conflicts from the time we are born to the time we die. We can't cover them all in this program as individual conflicts. I would have to write a hundred volumes to do that. However, with the tools you are learning here you can take care of most conflicts without too much trouble by designing your own strategies as you learn how your mind works.

Something important to consider at this point is your unconscious mind's ability to learn new strategies and present appropriate responses. Did you ever learn to ride a bicycle or to roller-blade or snow ski? At the beginning, it is always difficult. Without having practiced, the unconscious memory has no guidance in creating balance under the new circumstances. In each case, you are moving from a stable earth-bound platform that does not move, to one that does. Furthermore, but the new moving platform often doesn't seem to behave consistently!

It takes time for us to learn these activities to a point where they become automatic. Eventually, after having wobbled your way along on a bike for the first time and maybe fallen off a few times, your mind gets accustomed to all the movements and bumps and automatically compensates. You will get to the point where you throw your leg over the seat, push off, and start peddling. Everything else then becomes automatic, freeing your conscious mind to do other things that you regard as being more important. The part of the mind that does this for you is your unconscious memory system.

With the strategies you are learning in this program, the same thing is happening. The exercises you are working through are making your unconscious mind aware of how the strategies work and are giving it instructions to use those strategies. The more you use them, the easier it is for the unconscious to process them more and more quickly. I have trained dozens of people who eventually came to making the conscious/unconscious instruction process automatic.

Here is the process in a simple summary:

1. Understand that your unconscious mind "thinks" in terms of sensory devices such as sight, sound, touch, and emotion. Any system you use to communicate with it must use these prime methods.

2. Create a friendly awareness of your unconscious mind as a whole by being aware of an image or kinaesthetic awareness of an entity that can **represent** it for you. Be aware that its role is to protect you and will only provide apparently negative responses if it has no other strategy to give you.

3. Become aware of the strategy your mind uses to make you aware of the main emotions. Assess each method it uses by listing the visual and kinaesthetic characteristics of the

images and feelings it provides you with in conscious awareness. Get accustomed to analysing these methods.

4. Once you are clear on how your mind structures it's visual, kinaesthetic, auditory, smell and taste characteristics for strong positive beliefs and values, communicate your instructions to your unconscious mind by changing the characteristics of the strategies it has used for low energy beliefs to the characteristics used for strong beliefs. For instance, if a strong belief or value is expressed in terms of a fully surrounded 3D awareness, and the belief you want to change is expressed as a 2D flat image, change the 2D image to a 3D fully surrounded image. Map all the other characteristics such as colour intensity, feel and sound to conform to the strong belief characteristics. Add instruction to your unconscious representation to make the change permanent.

5. Learn to use your unique Neuro-Com strategy to change emotions and thought/feeling reactions. Practice them until your mind makes them automatic. Eventually your unconscious mind will take simple conscious instructions to do something and will automatically use the strategies you have taught it **to make the change instantly, without further conscious thought or energy**.

With this in mind, spend some time with the strategy used in the last exercise on self-image conflicts to take a look at other conflicts you may be aware of.

Try looking at:

- Sexual conflicts
- Money and wealth conflicts
- Religious conflicts

I chose these topics because they provide individuals and the human race with some of the most damaging sources of anxiety, anger, and guilt we are able to create.

As you take a look at these in yourself you may want to consider the following, which are based on thousands of clinical sessions I have been involved in over the years:

Sexual conflicts can be derived from several separate parts of the memory system that include:

- religious beliefs and training,
- parental views and the parent/child education session,
- social taboos, and
- the prime driver—good old natural (and honest) lust.

Money and wealth conflicts can be derived from:

- socially acceptable perceptions, or what society in general finds acceptable behaviour or levels of success,
- parental history and in-home teaching and awareness,
- jealousy,
- fear of success (self-image conflict), and
- greed based on social expectations.

Religious conflicts can be based on:

- religious education at church and school,
- the home environment and family history,
- mixed religion marriage of parents, and
- life's teachings introducing inconsistency and uncertainty ("How could God create such pain and suffering?")

As you move through each of these areas, you will meet some resistance to change because the emotional content of memory groups is so high for most of us. Almost all of our really strong values are derived from these three areas of life. If you do meet resistance to change, you will need to know how to modify your values system to reduce the level of emotional energy in the areas of conflict before you try to integrate them.

YOUR VALUES SYSTEM

Some of your belief systems carry more emotion in them than others. As memory groups that create your beliefs develop, specific thought/feeling reactions tend to attach higher levels of positive and negative emotions to each memory, until the overall emotional energy in the group makes it feel like a stronger belief system. It is these beliefs that create your Values system.

As an example that your unconscious will recognise easily, let's look at this in terms of pictures. Let's say you have two memory groups, each with the same number of memories. Over time, one memory group has absorbed more emotional energy:

Let your mind wander over the following images and ask your unconscious mind which one of these belief systems its world regards as carrying a greater level of value.

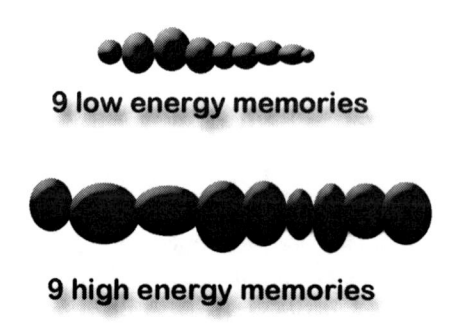

9 low energy memories

9 high energy memories

Figure 7. Comparison of energy levels in memory groups

Based on experience, I would be very surprised if you did not respond with a resounding "Belief Two." This is because the larger size is interpreted as having a greater level of strength or weight. In just the same way, memory groups are recognised by the characteristics with which they are encoded. We find that values, or high-energy belief systems, are encoded with specific patterns. Values that have higher levels of encoded energy or emotion tend to have a greater influence on our unconscious attitudes and hence our behaviours. If you change the pattern, the energy level in the belief is also changed.

Practical Neuro-Com

WHY ARE YOUR VALUES IMPORTANT?

Think about the things you have achieved during your lifetime. Think about the parts of your life and the people in it that make your life feel worthwhile. What is important to you and what qualities in yourself and the people around you do you rate highly?

Take some time and complete the next exercise by listing the people, places, and events that have given your life a sense of comfort or value. List these in the left-hand column of the forms on the next several pages.

Now think about the characteristics of each person, event, or place that has given it this sense of importance and list them in the right-hand column. Download and print several pages of these forms if necessary; indeed, the more you list, the better you will become aware of some of your own characteristics and drives.

This will be important when we start to create your future NeuroPrint in Chapter 7.

The people in my life I value	
Name	The characteristics I value

The places in my life that I value	
Place	The characteristics I value

The events in my life that I value	
Event	The characteristics I value

As you move through this exercise, you may notice that there seems to be something consistent in the things you value in each category. You may also notice that the things you value are similar between categories. The more time you spend on this exercise the more you will realise that you are truly programmed with a set of values that have directed every part of your life—the people to whom you are attracted, the places you go, and the things you do.

As you think about the results of your life, I'm going to ask you a question you may not want to answer with total honesty:

"Are you totally happy with the life you have, the people with whom you are surrounded, the job or business you have, the level of financial comfort?" Of course you are not. If you are happy, you probably wouldn't be putting the time and energy into this program.

Now consider this. Your entire life up to this point has been directed by the high-energy belief systems we know as values. Every thing, event, and person to which you are attracted and toward which you work is directed by your programming. Your future will continue down the same path unless you do two things.

1. Plan a change in future direction
2. Change your values to conform to and allow the evolution of your future as you design it.

Chapters 6 and 7 will lead you through an entire design program to create the future you want to create and to integrate the values you require to create it automatically.

Please make sure you understand everything we have studied to this point in the program. I suggest you now go back over the entire program to this point to revise and clarify your understanding of how your mind works and the elements of communicating with your unconscious mind. It is important that it is fresh in your mind as we begin the process of creating your future.

CHAPTER SIX

Designing Your Future

> **This chapter discusses:**
> - The Past—Present—Future
> - The design of your timeline
> - Your NeuroPrint
> - The role of emotional memory in developing your future
> - Embedded emotions, values, attitudes and their role in future behaviour
> - Creating balance in your future
> - Creating your Life Plan

PAST—PRESENT—FUTURE

We know that the PAST is the realm of your unconscious memory. Memories are stored in groups according to content with a cross-reference to when in the past the events happened.

NOW is the realm of consciousness. Consciousness does not exist at any time but right now, moment-by-moment. The last sentence is stored in the past unless you look back at it now. Consciousness controls the

The Neuro-Com Program

unconscious memory provided you are aware that most thought or feeling reactions that present themselves to you are coming from the memory. Only consciousness has the power to create something new.

So if the past is memory, and NOW is in consciousness, how does the mind process the future? Are we *really* in control of our future? Can we plan a future and be assured we can create something we want? The answer is a definite YES.

THE DESIGN OF YOUR TIMELINE

A useful way to understand how your mind works is to draw a line. Label one end the PAST. Label the other end FUTURE, and in the middle mark NOW.

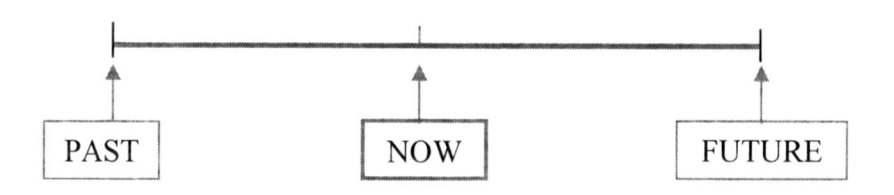

```
|────────────────|────────────────|
▲                ▲                ▲
|                |                |
[PAST]        [NOW]           [FUTURE]
```

Do you notice that when you consider this proposition that it seems natural to you? In other words, you tend to accept the idea about a past, a present, and a future without an internal argument because of the way that you have been programmed about the formation of time. We know what the past consists of and accept what now is, but what do you think the mind sees the future as? The only answer we have that makes sense is "future memory".

Your unconscious mind takes everything it has stored in the past, all the events, emotions, and book learning it has ever encountered. On the basis of the way your past has evolved and the progression of events, your unconscious mind projects a likely future. It does so to make sure there are not too many surprises and that it can protect you adequately.

Does this mean our future is laid down, and we can't change it? No, not at all. Your future projection is the most likely possibility at any point in time, based on your past experience of similar events. If anything

Designing Your Future

changes in the past memory, such as deleting an emotion or even a complete memory, the future projection of your unconscious mind will be moulded to take this into account. Any conscious intervention in NOW also changes the future projection. We know this is the most likely scenario because of the thousands of people with whom we have worked who have performed a simple experiment. Without any prompting or advice on what was likely to happen, I have asked hundreds of clients to become aware of their timeline and move along it into their future. To their amazement and shock, they found themselves moving through a series of future memories that appeared as real as past memories. Invariably, the future projections seemed to be consistent with their past experience, with a few minor changes based on possibilities. These possibilities are based on recent life experience, knowledge, and hopes.

This methodology was originally developed by Tad James, a psychotherapist with long experience in Neuro-Linguistic Programming. His development of understanding of the timeline led to some of the most powerful methods of change ever developed in therapy. The concept gave us access to methods of changing the past by taking the emotion out of entire memory groups. The most amazing effect of this was that the future timeline changes before your eyes.

With practical experience with thousands of individuals, it became clear that the unconscious mind could represent itself in a way that is easily understood and with which you can work. As the development of the methodology evolved, we started to see the relationships of values and emotional content of memory in a new light. It became possible to delete negative emotions from entire memory groups and watch the effect on the future program within moments. It became possible to negotiate with individual parts of the memory to create a positive outcome on the entire past memory with the immediate release of internal stressors. And, it was possible to move inside a causal memory to find the emotion and remove it without having to know the events contained in the memory! In other words, it is not necessary to explore old traumatic memories repeatedly in order to remove either the emotion from a memory or the decisions the unconscious mind has made to behave in a particular way.

The power of the timeline concept should not be underestimated, and you must understand clearly its use before you venture down that road. This current program will provide you with all the necessary tools to get yourself ready to use the method. Actually preparing for and using the timeline requires a complete training program on its own. This is impractical to do as part of this particular program. However, I will show you how to create balance in your life and adjust your values system to be congruent with your future life plan, your NeuroPrint.

YOUR NEUROPRINT

The future timeline I have explained is what I call a NeuroPrint. Your NeuroPrint is a future memory projection created from your entire life history. It is fluid (changes in detail) and is programmable by conscious intervention.

Most people who take the time to work through this program want to do two things:

1. Feel better about themselves
2. Find a way to create a new future

We have covered several powerful strategies to use in feeling better about yourself and for taking control of how your unconscious mind works for you. Now we turn our attention to designing the NeuroPrint or the future life YOU want and putting everything in place to ensure its outcome. William James, the father of modern psychology stated the following with great insight in 1896:

"Your attitude at the beginning of any endeavour guarantees its outcome." In other words, what your unconscious thinks and feels is appropriate when you begin something is what you actually get.

The events that direct your life are controlled primarily by your values system, which in turn controls your attitudes and behaviours. These are the things that expose you to other people and determine how they react to you. In this life, no man or woman is an island—we all depend on others to some extent, and we need to be able to positively influence them to support our endeavors.

As we have already seen, the flow of controlling mechanisms in memory is that embedded emotions create values, which in turn create attitudes; subsequently, attitudes create future behaviour.

On the surface it would seem two things direct what life brings to us:

1. Our own internal drives to create the environment we want.

2. The way others react to us if they are in a position to influence our position in life.

If we don't have any particular drive to create anything more than just existing, then we won't go out of our way to set forth and create anything. We will have no motivation strong enough to overcome our built-in lethargy or fears.

If our built-in program causes us to exhibit behaviours toward other people or situations that are perceived by other people as inconsistent with the desired behaviour, we will not be given a chance to demonstrate we are capable. Usually the two behavioural areas are related.

For example, an individual comes from a poor home in which the father rarely works or is in a low-paying job. This situation lowers his self-esteem. The mother stays at home making do and justifying the meagre existence to herself and her family. The parents watch television at night and are constantly making comments about the "fat cats" who are making all the money, leaving them with little. The individual grows up with a belief system that being poor is okay and that being wealthy will draw some negative reactions from his peers.

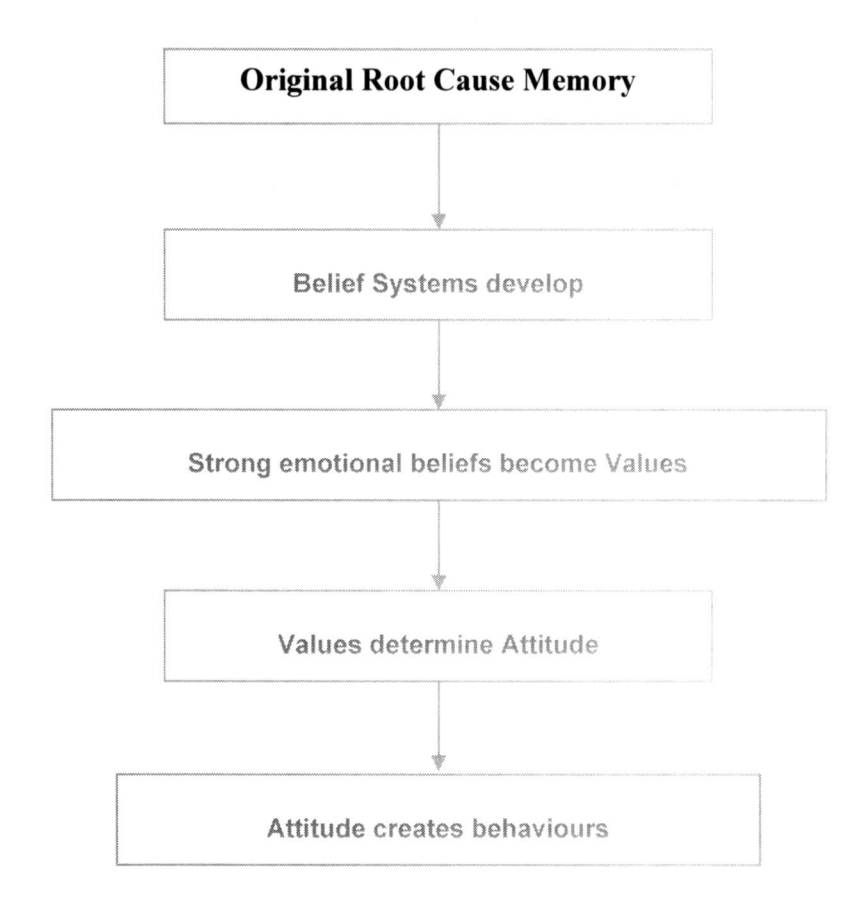

```
┌─────────────────────────────────┐
│   **Original Root Cause Memory**    │
└─────────────────────────────────┘
                 │
                 ▼
┌─────────────────────────────────┐
│     Belief Systems develop      │
└─────────────────────────────────┘
                 │
                 ▼
┌─────────────────────────────────────┐
│ Strong emotional beliefs become Values │
└─────────────────────────────────────┘
                 │
                 ▼
┌─────────────────────────────────┐
│   Values determine Attitude     │
└─────────────────────────────────┘
                 │
                 ▼
┌─────────────────────────────────┐
│   Attitude creates behaviours   │
└─────────────────────────────────┘
```

Figure 8. The creation of our behaviours

These belief systems create a values system that results in an aggressive attitude toward people that have money or are in a position of power. When the child of this family presents him- or herself to the manager of a company for a job, the unconscious behaviour will show some level of aggression and poor self-esteem. All the behaviours being exhibited would convey a lack of respect, even if the individual tried to take on a different role. What chance do you think this person has of getting hired?

In this way, we constantly sabotage ourselves. Our unconscious mind takes what it has learned about appropriate behaviour and uses it to create the outcomes of our life.

The same scenario applies to every area of life. Relationships, for example, are often sabotaged by our language or behaviour at critical times. We say something we don't consciously mean or do something stupid when a slightly different way of speaking or acting would have created heaven for us. All of this happens because our unconscious mind has a belief that we don't deserve to have this person in our lives.

Sometimes we have an opportunity to allow change to be placed before us, and our unconscious program ensures that something happens that stops us from being in the right place at the right time.

Your program will continue to do this until you die unless you make a conscious effort to change it.

Creating the Plan

The exercises used over Chapters 6 and 7 will help you create a future plan in a format that your unconscious mind understands and on which it will act. It may appear to be a lot of effort to you at the moment, but the results you will achieve will be spectacular. I have taken hundreds of people through this process and still get letters of thanks from my clients for helping them create a fantastic future.

The steps you will take are:

1. Creating a future plan that is balanced
2. Creating your 10-year plan
3. Creating your 5-year plan
4. Creating your 1-year plan
5. Creating your 6-month plan
6. Determine the values required to create your NeuroPrints effectively
7. Analyse the patterns of your values and modify them to suit your desired future
8. Integrate your values and plans
9. Install the new NeuroPrint in your future timeline

1. CREATING BALANCE IN YOUR FUTURE

Many of us get so focused on a particular event or person in our future that we forget to think about all the other aspects of our life. The result is that we lose some things we regard as precious.

I love to tell the story of the salesman who decided to find out how to create a different, very successful life. He found a specialist in setting goals so he could become focussed clearly on making money. The exercise was so successful that he started to make big money. As his bank balanced registered his first million dollars, he reset his goals and aimed for five million, then ten, then fifty. Soon, he was wealthy enough for his wife to afford the best lawyers in the world to sue for divorce and take him for everything he had earned! He forgot about the other important areas of his life and lost everything.

The moral of the story is, of course, that it is very foolish to concentrate all your efforts in only one area of your life. You must create balance so that each main area of your life can support the others in a healthy way.

Next you will find an exercise that will become the foundation of your future NeuroPrint. It is so important that I suggest you do not go any further in this program until you complete it and understand its significance.

Exercise: Your life as it is

Put a cross on each arm of the star below at a point relating to the level of energy you **currently** put into that area of life. A cross at 10 indicates a very high level of energy; a cross at 0 means you put no energy into it.

Designing Your Future

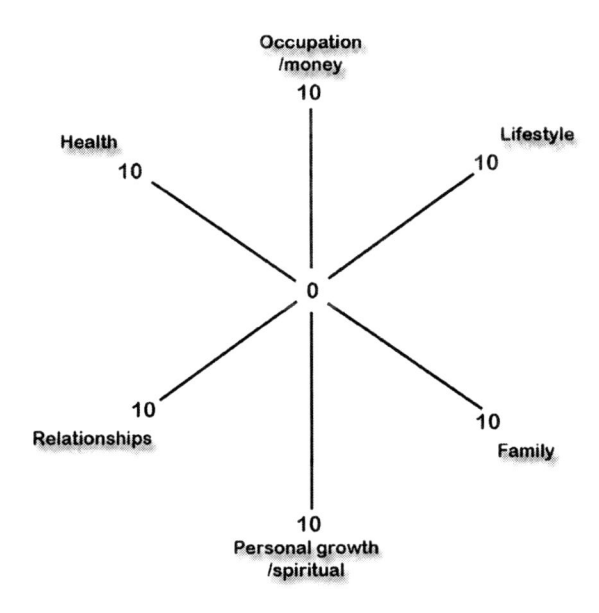

```
              Occupation
               /money
                 10
Health                      Lifestyle
  10                          10
    \         |         /
     \        |        /
      \       |       /
       \      |      /
        \    0     /
        /     |    \
       /      |     \
      /       |      \
     10       |       10
Relationships |       Family
              |
              10
        Personal growth
          /spiritual
```

Figure 9. Establishing where you stand now in balance

Now join the crosses you have placed on the chart with a single line in the closest you can create or approximate a circle.

Do you seem to have some flat spots in your circle? Most people do and that's okay for now. The ideal situation in a balanced life would be to create a perfect circle. In designing your future, you should take this into consideration.

2. CREATING YOUR 10-YEAR PLAN

To design a new future that is congruent (consistent) right from the very beginning, you need to understand the big picture before you design the little bits in between. It is pointless planning to take one step in front of you, and then another, and then another if you don't know that your final destination is in the opposite direction!

Why are you alive? Why do you keep getting up in the morning year after year after year? Think about this for a minute with a view to discovering what you really want in this life. You have the chance now to fulfil your dreams and, if you wish, contribute to the welfare of the human race.

There are certain rules that need to be followed to ensure your future is congruent. We are about to embark on an exercise to design the future precisely as you want it to be. I am sure you have heard about the importance of goal-setting a thousand times. Very few people do it, however, and those that do usually see goal-setting as being limited to only a few months out into the future. The exercise we will do is to design a LIFE Plan or what I call a NeuroPrint.

This exercise requires us to ensure that what we do will make the unconscious mind sit up and take notice. We want it to act on our instructions and actually create the life we plan. For it to do this, we must ensure that the instructions we give it will meet little or no resistance and that everyone in our life is catered for adequately. Make your goals ecologically sound within your own environment. This means, simply, do you really want them?

Your goals create balance in your life so they are sustainable over a long period.

THE RULES OF DESIGNING GOOD GOALS

As you consider the goals you will write during these exercises, consider each goal against this checklist:

Are you sure YOU really want it? Often, we set a goal for ourselves because someone else thinks it is a good idea or it is considered socially desirable. If YOU don't really want it for yourself don't set it as a goal—you will probably never pursue it.

Is everyone involved in creating the goal adequately catered for? In other words, will the goal fulfil the needs of those people you care about or to whom you have an obligation? Will they be happy with the result? Here you need to decide if you want particular people in your life or if you really want to create the outcome even if it won't suit other people in your life.

Is the goal couched in simple terms? If it isn't, you will find you will not be able to create a simple image or awareness of the goal. It will be difficult to instruct your mind to create it. Reword or reconfigure the goal so you can create a comfortable and clear awareness of it, both visually and kinaesthetically.

Is it measurable? Your goal must be specific regarding what you are trying to achieve. This is not as important for the 10-year goals and beyond because we often only have a vague awareness of some outcomes. Still, the more accurately you can see the goal, the easier it will be to create it.

Is it realistic? Can the goal really be achieved in the time you have allocated for it? Be liberal here because you will find your unconscious mind is capable of providing behaviours that will speed up creating the goal. You will often find that a goal you develop will have another part of the mind try to shout you down and say you are being stupid for thinking so big. Write it down anyway. As you proceed with the next steps, you will see at a logical level if it is possible or not.

Have you put a date on it? Write down the completion date as part of the goal.

Is the goal positive? Your unconscious mind cannot create an awareness of something that is negative without conscious logic. It will interpret things in the simplest way possible, and negative language creates confusion. For example, think of a ball that is NOT red. What do you see? The first thing that will appear to you is a red ball until you modify it through logic. So, be very wary of negative language! If you can't see the outcome, you may be using negative language to try to describe it.

What beliefs and values are required to allow your unconscious mind to create the goal? We will deal with this aspect in Chapter 7. It is very important to ensure your belief system is congruent with creating the goal. In this situation, you will modify the energy level in your beliefs to suit the goals you really want.

WRITING YOUR LIFE PLAN

The next few pages feature forms that will help you decide what kind of a life you wish to create, first from the perspective of the "big picture"

10 years from now, then to break down those targets into smaller and smaller bites. Print as many pages as you need to create a fulfilling life.

You may also chose to use your Learning Journal for this process. Your Learning Journal should become a constant companion in your journey and contain your Life Plan, your NeuroPrint and your evaluation of how your mind responds to the changes you are making. It is a valuable resource in designing and evolving your new future, so treat it with value. If you don't place importance on your future, why should your unconscious mind treat it with any more importance than planning your next meal?

Important reminder about 10-year goals

When looking at your 10-year plan, your unconscious mind may suggest that such goals are either impossible or YOU cannot create them. This will happen if you hesitate to write them down or you have a negative emotional response to them. Disregard such reactions, and write them down anyway! Such reactions are simply your unconscious programs telling you that either you have never done something as big before or that your self-image is such that your mind does not believe you can create them. In other words, your values system thinks the goal is ridiculous based on its current program. Ignore this and write down the goal anyway. You will be shown how to modify your values system to accommodate creating the goal.

As you start to determine your 5-year goals, ensure that some of them will lead you to complete the 10-year goals. This is a logical progression. For example, if one of your goals is to be a brain surgeon in 10 years, then the logical progression is that you must at least be significantly through, or have completed, medical school in five years. Or, if your 10-year goal is to be retired, how much money will you need or what plans do you need to have in place in five years to make the 10-year goal viable? These are logical questions to ask.

For each of your 10-year goals, you will have a series of pre-conditions to be met in five years that need to be either completed or well under way for the 10 year goals to be created. In addition to these five-year goals, there will be many that can be completed over the next five years that do not need 10 years for creation. Include these 5 year achievable goals in your listing.

Similarly, ensure that some of your one-year goals will lead to creating your five-year goals and so on. In this way, the initial stages of your plan will be totally congruent and mutually supportive—each stage supports the next.

It is also important to ensure that each of the life areas you reviewed in "Creating Balance" is considered. Include goals relating to family, relationships, income, health and lifestyle, and personal growth to ensure you receive maximum benefit from the process. Only you can determine what is important to you. It is okay if your wheel is out of balance in the short term if, for example, you need to concentrate on creating income for a while. Just don't forget to include the people you need in your life and those who are important to you.

Whether you use a your Learning Journal or just use these forms, allocate some alone time and ensure you are undisturbed during this process. Remember, you are not just planning your next holiday—you are planning the rest of your life!

Remember: Always start with the goals furthest out, in this case 10 years. Defining the remaining goals then becomes a logical exercise of what you need to do or complete in each earlier period that logically lead toward the later goal.

Also, do not be phased if when you start writing your 10 year goals if your unconscious mind starts giving you the feel that some of these goals are not achievable. If you have never done it before your unconscious belief system has no measuring stick to measure the result by, so it will tend to tell you it can't be done. Ignore it. If a desired goal comes to mind, write it down anyway. By the time you have logically worked through the required 5 year and 1 year goals, your mind will already be seeing that your 10 year goals are possible.

It is only if the 1 year and 6 month goals are still unrealistic for some of your 10 year outcomes that you may have to rethink the realities of the initial 10 year goals.

NEUROPRINT GOALS FOR MY 10-YEAR PLAN

....
....
....
....
....
....
....
....
....
....
....
....
....
....
....
....
....
....
....
....

NEUROPRINT GOALS FOR MY 5-YEAR PLAN

NEUROPRINT GOALS FOR MY ONE-YEAR PLAN

....
....
....
....
....
....
....
....
....
....
....
....
....
....
....
....
....
....
....
....

NEUROPRINT GOALS FOR MY SIX-MONTH PLAN

Have you found this process difficult? Many people do because they have never tried to plan their entire future. Many people put more time, emotion, and effort into designing their annual holiday than they do designing their life. I guess most of us are looking for the quick fix or short-term gratification that we believe we can achieve immediately. What they don't realize is that by spending the time to design their entire life, the so-called quick fixes automatically become their life. Their unconscious mind takes over the control of creating a satisfying life.

The exercise you have just completed is not designed as a one-off event. I suggest that reviewing your goals should be a regular part of life. As your life evolves, it is important to sit down every three to six months and plan the next six months. Each time, ensure that what you are creating conforms to the direction of your long-term plans. If you decide you wish to change your medium- or long-term plans, it is as simple as drawing up a new NeuroPrint and installing it.

Remember: Your future timeline is fluid and can be changed at will.

What do you need to value?

Now that you know how to create a direction for the future, you need to turn your attention to another aspect that is critical to creating your future. As we have discussed, your values need to be congruent with creating the future you want. That is not always the case.

Exercise: Values assessment

The exercises you complete in this chapter will be an eye-opener for most people. It is important that you complete this values exercise, no matter what resistance your unconscious mind presents. Your understanding of this process will determine how successful you are at programming your new NeuroPrint.

As we have discussed, your values system comprises a series of beliefs that have recorded higher than average emotional content or level of importance. This means they will always present to you as beliefs about a range of subjects that would motivate most people to discuss and expound upon their view. When you think about it, it is essentially values that create most arguments and even wars.

In this exercise, we you are going to take a look at the ideas, people, and things you value about each area of life you examined when we investigated the level of balance in your life. Those areas are:

Occupation / money

Lifestyle

Family

Relationships

Health

Personal development / spirituality

I have arranged these in no particular order of importance. The importance will vary depending on the program you have taken on board. HOW you treat their importance will tend to determine what you do with your life. Think now about the order that is important to you by numbering them from 1 to 6 in the margin. Then, look back at your balance star and notice which of the life areas were rated as having more energy devoted to them. Do you notice any similarities?

Over the next six pages you will find one form for each life area. Go through each page and in the LEFT-hand column list the things you value and regard as important to you for that life area. Don't try to list them in any order; just record them as they come to you. There is room for 12 values, but you may have only a few in certain areas. In other areas, you may have more such that you'll need to print several pages. Write down what flows. After you have completed this exercise, I will describe what comes next.

Things I Value about my Relationships

List as they come to you	#	Re-list in order of energy
	1	
	2	
	3	
	4	
	5	
	6	
	7	
	8	
	9	
	10	
	11	
	12	

Designing Your Future

Things I Value about my Health

List as they come to you		Re-list in order of energy
	1	
	2	
	3	
	4	
	5	
	6	
	7	
	8	
	9	
	10	
	11	
	12	

Things I Value about my Spiritual Life

List as they come to you		Re-list in order of energy
	1	
	2	
	3	
	4	
	5	
	6	
	7	
	8	
	9	
	10	
	11	
	12	

Things I Value about my Occupation

List as they come to you		Re-list in order of energy
	1	
	2	
	3	
	4	
	5	
	6	
	7	
	8	
	9	
	10	
	11	
	12	

Things I Value about my Lifestyle

List as they come to you		Re-list in order of energy
	1	
	2	
	3	
	4	
	5	
	6	
	7	
	8	
	9	
	10	
	11	
	12	

Things I Value about my Family

List as they come to you		Re-list in order of energy
	1	
	2	
	3	
	4	
	5	
	6	
	7	
	8	
	9	
	10	
	11	
	12	

As you completed this exercise, you may have noticed that some areas of your life were more difficult to list than others. This occurs because your unconscious program has recorded different levels of energy in the belief systems surrounding that area of life. Areas with significantly greater areas of energy allow you to list more values more quickly.

Next, we'll start to assess the values you have listed in order of their importance. This requires a little more input and an awareness of your feelings about each value.

Consider each list one at a time. Slowly read through your list and get a feel for the amount of energy in each value. Some will feel the same but may have other characteristics that differentiate them for you. The goal is to, using the right column on the form, re-list the values in order of their perceived level of energy, that is, their level of importance to YOU. This is an intuitive process in a way since you will get a "gut" reaction as to their importance to you by how they make you feel. As an example, for the topic of Occupation, let's say a some of the values you listed were Money, Enjoyment, Security, Friendship. Now when you access each of these as to how they make you feel, if you were to measure that feeling on a positive scale of 1-10 where 10 represents a really strong positive and supportive feeling, which of these values come up the highest? Take your time and ensure that they seem to be in the right order for you.

Don't be surprised if the way your values feel are not in order you might logically think would be useful in that life area. Remember, your unconscious programs are just that, programs. They are not necessarily logical as to how they deal with day to day life. They react and give you emotional and thought reactions based on what they have been told are valid reactions. We will deal with this discrepancy in the next chapter.

Important: Never ask someone else for help with this exercise. You need to know what YOU believe is important. Getting assistance from others will only inflict their beliefs on you. This is the exact situation you are trying to change in this program!

In the next chapter, we will begin to discover powerful ways to assess which values are required to produce certain outcomes. You will discover how to modify the energy in some values so that your unconscious mind will actually act on creating the goals you have listed, doing so automatically and without further conscious input. You will be in control of your future.

CHAPTER SEVEN

Designing Future Memory

> **This chapter discusses:**
>
> - Balancing values with goals
> - Designing future memory projections
> - Creating future projections that are congruent with your values
> - Changing values and attitudes to be congruent with future projections
> - Programming the future so you create success automatically

BALANCING VALUES WITH GOALS

If you have diligently followed the exercises in this program and understand the relationship between beliefs, values, attitudes, and behaviour you will now be aware that the relationship between values and creating your goals is critical.

You can consciously plan whatever future you want. You can seek wealth, amazing relationships, loving family environments, spiritual enlightenment, and perfect health. But **if your unconscious mind has been programmed NOT to value these things, your goals are nothing but idle dreams.**

In the process you completed in Chapter 6, you laid out a future game plan that you desire. You went to great lengths to ensure your goals list was congruent for the next 10 years and made sure that each goal fulfilled the design criteria for Ecological Goals. Ensure the goals are what you really want, everyone is accounted for, your goals are simple, and they are timed appropriately.

Now we will undergo a process to determine the values required to make each of your goals achievable and, if necessary, modify the energy level in the required value to make the goal achievable.

IMPORTANT LEARNING YOU SHOULD UNDERSTAND

Before proceeding, spend some time reviewing the following:

- Your understanding of how your unconscious memory has been programmed.
- How your mind creates its belief and values systems.
- The relationship between values and their external representations, attitude, and behaviour.
- Your awareness of your friendly, unconscious mind and the images/feelings associated with communicating with him/her/it.
- Your method of seeing, feeling, or hearing your internal unconscious processes.
- Knowing that your unconscious mind does not communicate with you in language as a rule, but through the visual and kinaesthetic clues with which it presents us.

Now you are ready to proceed.

MAKING GOALS CONGRUENT WITH YOUR VALUES

Your unconscious mind processes information in visual images, sounds, and emotions. It "codes" the levels of importance of specific incoming information in a way that is consistent, in general, between belief systems by varying the level or type of emotion stored in the memory groups or by changing the patterns it uses to describe the images of the physical awareness it embeds in the memory.

The way that your unconscious mind encodes this information will vary the way you perceive your surrounding circumstances and the amount of importance you place on events. That is, your awareness of a particular event in consciousness (NOW) will tend to be changed by the thought or feeling reaction being presented by your unconscious in response. Past memory group encoding responds to incoming sensory clues relating to it, presenting fragments of past events and attached emotions back to conscious mind. These fragments in turn change your awareness of what is actually happening, and in some cases can make you see, hear or experience the event very differently to the reality. Such past associations can, and do, change your reactions to your environment and your behaviour

The result is that when a certain event happens in your life, your unconscious mind may discard it as being unimportant. Consequently, you will not react to it. On the other hand, if conscious mind scans your unconscious memory and finds a belief or memory group associated with the event that contains "important" coding, then it will prompt you to notice and act on the event. Your response may range from a self-protective device to simply a change in the dilation of your pupils or a change in skin colour to attract someone you have just met. It will tend to happen automatically if your mind believes it can fulfil its highest intent by doing so.

A practical example of this occurs in relationships. You meet someone for the first time and take in all the sensory clues surrounding that person. It sees the details of their body shape, hair colour, eyes, clothing, and jewellery. It also perceives the way they walk, talk, and the subliminal clues they are sending, including pheromones (sexual attractant hormones) released into the atmosphere. If the patterns they present match those that your unconscious mind has recorded as being desirable, you will be strongly attracted to that person. If it does not find an association or finds a negative association with something in the way this person looks or acts, you may be repelled or angered by your new acquaintance.

The same rules apply to moving into a situation or meeting someone who can help you make money, find happiness, or create excellent health. Your unconscious mind will attract you to or repel you from any person or event based on what it "knows" in its recorded belief and values system. It all depends on how the memory has been encoded.

By changing the way this information is encoded, you can change the level of importance that your mind places on relevant data so that it is more consistent with your goals. For example, if one of your goals is to have $30,000 in the bank by the end of the year, but you had placed a very low value on money or wealth when you elicited your values for career, do you think your mind will create the conditions to satisfactorily complete this goal? It's not very likely, is it?

Now suppose we change how the value of money has been encoded so that its level of importance to the mind is enhanced. In fact, we increase the importance of the value so that it is now on top of the list. That makes money, or wealth, far more compelling to the mind and dramatically increases the chance you will reach your goal.

We make these changes to the value system by changing the image or feeling that is encoded into the value. You will be shown how to do this in this segment of the program. Then, using forms on the next few pages, you will modify the values you need for your top five goals to make them consistent with creating those goals. Once you have practised the procedure on the top five goals you want to create, you will find it easier and easier to do the same for every goal.

Exercise: Matching Values to Goals

The following process should be followed exactly. It is designed to match the way your mind has encoded your values to the way it has encoded your goals. By doing this exercise, your goals will be virtually irresistible to your mind, and it will use all its vast resources to create them.

1. Complete an evaluation of your goals for six months through to 10 years as we have done in Chapter 6. Ensure you have read the section on *The Rules of Designing Good Goals* before you do this!

2. Read the section "Your Value System in Chapter 5", then think about the things you value in each of the five life

areas—the things that are important to you. **Note: Your values are NOT usually your goals**. As you think of them, write them in the left-hand column of the relevant table headed "Things I Value about my ...." in Chapter 6.

3. Now, re-list these values in their order of importance to your mind in the next column, by the way they "feel". You were shown how to evaluate their order of importance at the end of Chapter 6.

4. Now turn to the "Neuro-Com Characteristics Checklist" forms that follow this, one for each life area. For each of the top three values you determined as important for each life area that you have previously determined in (3), space is provided to give a brief (one or two word) description of the visual image or awareness that comes to your mind when you think of each value. For example, a value of "closeness" for the life area of Relationships may bring to mind an image of two people holding each other. You will notice the similarity of these forms with the forms you used in Chapter 5 to determine your mind's method of encoding characteristics in emotions. In this situation, we use the same method.

Let's say, for example, that the top-rated values for Occupation are listed as:

- Appreciation of the value of money
- Desire for recognition
- Friendships

Yours may be different. Don't be swayed by my selection—we are just looking at the principals involved here. When I go inside my own mind to see how I perceive the appreciation of the value of money, my mind comes back with a picture of a pile of bank notes sitting on a timber pallet. The contents of the picture are unimportant, but what I perceive to be the characteristics of this image are as follows:

I am in the picture. That is it is panoramic 360 degrees around me.

The Neuro-Com Program

> *It is sharp and very clear.*
>
> *The image of the money is colourful, while the background is grey.*
>
> *It is a movie. I am moving toward the pile of cash.*
>
> *The picture feels warm and comfortable.*
>
> *My internal physical awareness is one of excitement with some tightening of the stomach muscles.*
>
> *The picture has a feeling of lightness with an awareness of large size.*
>
> *I can hear a sharp rattling sound like money being counted with a muffled babble of voices in the background.*
>
> *I can taste a metallic, coppery taste.*

In this exercise, I would enter these characteristics under the Value 1 column on the sheet for Occupation. I then look at the second value on my Occupation list, and follow the same process, followed by the third. Because these register as the top values for this particular life area, they are likely to have similarities among them.

Then turn to the next life area, Lifestyle, and repeat the process for the top three values for Lifestyle. Work through each life area in turn. Take your time and become comfortable with the methods. The more you do this exercise, the easier it becomes as your unconscious mind learns the process. What you are doing in reality is teaching your unconscious mind how it has learned in the past and giving it some powerful tools to help you in the future.

Note: Because of the format of this book and the limited space to provide these forms, more extensive forms are available from our website. Go to http://www.neuro-com.org/downloads/ to download, print and use these more useful forms.

Neuro-Com Characteristics Checklist - Occupation

	Value 1	Value 2	Value 3
Visual			
Self in or out of picture			
Framed or panoramic view			
Bright or dull			
Black and white or colour			
Three dimensional or flat			
Sharply focussed or blurred			
Movie or still image			
Number of pictures (if stills)			
Intensity of colour			
Feelings / kinaesthetic			
Warm, cool, or cold			
Texture – rough / smooth			
Vibration – mild / intense			
Intensity of feeling			
Size			
Shape			
Weight			
Movement			
Steady or intermittent			
Internal or external			
Pressure			
Auditory			
Volume			
Pitch			
Direction			
Tone			
Rhythm			
Smell			
Taste			

Neuro-Com Characteristics Checklist - Lifestyle

	Value 1	Value 2	Value 3
Visual			
Self in or out of picture			
Framed or panoramic view			
Bright or dull			
Black and white or colour			
Three dimensional or flat			
Sharply focussed or blurred			
Movie or still image			
Number of pictures (if stills)			
Intensity of colour			
Feelings / kinaesthetic			
Warm, cool, or cold			
Texture – rough / smooth			
Vibration – mild / intense			
Intensity of feeling			
Size			
Shape			
Weight			
Movement			
Steady or intermittent			
Internal or external			
Pressure			
Auditory			
Volume			
Pitch			
Direction			
Tone			
Rhythm			
Smell			
Taste			

Neuro-Com Characteristics Checklist - Relationships

	Value 1	Value 2	Value 3
Visual			
Self in or out of picture			
Framed or panoramic view			
Bright or dull			
Black and white or colour			
Three dimensional or flat			
Sharply focussed or blurred			
Movie or still image			
Number of pictures (if stills)			
Intensity of colour			
Feelings / kinaesthetic			
Warm, cool, or cold			
Texture – rough / smooth			
Vibration – mild / intense			
Intensity of feeling			
Size			
Shape			
Weight			
Movement			
Steady or intermittent			
Internal or external			
Pressure			
Auditory			
Volume			
Pitch			
Direction			
Tone			
Rhythm			
Smell			
Taste			

Neuro-Com Characteristics Checklist - Family

	Value 1	Value 2	Value 3
Visual			
Self in or out of picture			
Framed or panoramic view			
Bright or dull			
Black and white or colour			
Three dimensional or flat			
Sharply focussed or blurred			
Movie or still image			
Number of pictures (if stills)			
Intensity of colour			
Feelings / kinaesthetic			
Warm, cool, or cold			
Texture – rough / smooth			
Vibration – mild / intense			
Intensity of feeling			
Size			
Shape			
Weight			
Movement			
Steady or intermittent			
Internal or external			
Pressure			
Auditory			
Volume			
Pitch			
Direction			
Tone			
Rhythm			
Smell			
Taste			

Neuro-Com Characteristics Checklist - Health

	Value 1	Value 2	Value 3
Visual			
Self in or out of picture			
Framed or panoramic view			
Bright or dull			
Black and white or colour			
Three dimensional or flat			
Sharply focussed or blurred			
Movie or still image			
Number of pictures (if stills)			
Intensity of colour			
Feelings / kinaesthetic			
Warm, cool, or cold			
Texture – rough / smooth			
Vibration – mild / intense			
Intensity of feeling			
Size			
Shape			
Weight			
Movement			
Steady or intermittent			
Internal or external			
Pressure			
Auditory			
Volume			
Pitch			
Direction			
Tone			
Rhythm			
Smell			
Taste			

Neuro-Com Characteristics Checklist - Spiritual

	Value 1	Value 2	Value 3
Visual			
Self in or out of picture			
Framed or panoramic view			
Bright or dull			
Black and white or colour			
Three dimensional or flat			
Sharply focussed or blurred			
Movie or still image			
Number of pictures (if stills)			
Intensity of colour			
Feelings / kinaesthetic			
Warm, cool, or cold			
Texture – rough / smooth			
Vibration – mild / intense			
Intensity of feeling			
Size			
Shape			
Weight			
Movement			
Steady or intermittent			
Internal or external			
Pressure			
Auditory			
Volume			
Pitch			
Direction			
Tone			
Rhythm			
Smell			
Taste			

EVALUATING YOUR RESULTS

You may have already become aware of what is happening when you complete this exercise. Let's look at the processes that are becoming obvious by comparing:

- The two Life Areas that showed up as most important to you when you completed the Life Balance Star
- The three top values for each of these two Life Areas
- The values characteristics for the Life Areas of lowest energy input

Typically, what we find is that the characteristics used to encode the values in the Life Areas into which we put the most energy are very similar. For example, you may find that your mind always encodes these as panoramic movies that are clear and colourful. Or, if you tend to process the information kinaesthetically, you may find they are all feelings of warmth and lightness and are located in your chest with a pulsing sensation.

The way your unconscious mind has encoded these values tends to be the same. Your unconscious mind processes its recorded programs with the level of logic that says, "If it is IMPORTANT, this is how we encode it." In other words, your mind records high energy belief and values with similar or identical encoding in everything that it regards as important.

When you start to look at the way values are encoded for Life Areas that have not had significant energy put into them, you may start to find significant variations. If you normally process information visually, for example, you may find the pictures are just still postcards rather than the panoramic movies used for high-energy values. You may find you don't even get a picture.

Now look at it from the perspective of your unconscious mind. It will create behaviours based on what it perceives to be levels of importance. If the encoding it uses for a low-energy value stops it from doing anything, you can start to see why you spend so little time in those Life Areas or events. A simple example of this is someone who has low levels of energy recorded in the value of remembering birthdays. Do you think his/her unconscious mind will prompt when a partner's birthday passes without remembering it? That particular encoding could get you into a lot of trouble and may be worth changing!

WHAT DO I NEED TO VALUE?

On the basis of the last exercise you can understand why most people can write down their goals 'till the cows come home but never create them unless they really value the outcome. Over the years, dealing with hundreds of people who have been told to write down their goals, and those goals will magically be fulfilled, very few get the results they want. They have left out an important step in the process—getting their unconscious mind to support creating the desired goal.

To do this, we need to know *what we need to value* to have our unconscious mind actually treat a desired goal as serious. This step requires some conscious, logical thought from you to match desirable values to the goals you have set yourself.

In the following exercise we are now going to show you the reverse of what we have just done. You are now going to see what has to be done to actually reprogram your values to be gongruent with your desired goals. Doing this will make your mind sit up and take notice of its new instruction to create goals that it may have ignored in the past. This is powerful!

Exercise: Matching Desired Goals with Required Values

1. Turn to the forms headed "**Values Needed to Create a ………..Goal**" and write a brief description of **your most important goal** in each Life Area at the top of the page. If you don't have a goal in one particular area then use two from another area. Remember, these are goals in life that are logically important to you. For example, they may be important from the perspective of how they affect other people you care about, such as income security or health.

2. Think of the things that you logically need to VALUE in order to achieve each goal. Write the six or seven most important values in the appropriate section. Note: They may differ from the values you listed for this Life Area in previous exercises! These Values are ones that you would logically need in order to create the goal you are working on. As an example, if you had a goal of owning a mansion overlooking the Mediterranean in the south of France, do you think you might need to have some significant level of value for stable income? Now number them in order of importance.

3. Take the THREE MOST IMPORTANT VALUES you listed for each goal, and using similar descriptions given as a guide on the "Value Characteristics Checklist," describe the characteristics of the images or awareness brought to mind as you consider these top three values and record them in the forms entitled "Neuro-Com Characteristics Checklist – Goal Creation".

4. Compare the descriptions of these values to the characteristics given for the top two values given for each Life Area. In other words do the characteristics you are aware of in these "logically required values" match the characteristics of your unconscious high energy values? Do they vary significantly?

If they do your unconscious mind probably does not place enough importance on them to create your goals. As you work through these exercises you will soon notice that even small variations in the characteristics make a huge difference in the level of importance your mind places on them. For example, let's say your mind uses a three dimensional view of a high value or memory with you actually in the scene and seeing it with your own eyes. That perception installs very high levels of positive "feel" to it. Just a small change like pulling away from your position so you also see yourself in the picture as opposed to seeing the environment as though you were actually there, can change the energy in the picture in a big way.

Next, change the image or awareness of each value so that it matches the characteristics of the top values in each life area. At the same time keep in your mind the awareness that you are asking your mind to recode the values needed to create the goals so that they have a high priority.

5. Notice that as you re-evaluate your goals, do they seem to be more compelling to you now? I'm suspecting you'll find that they do, do they not? Keep the new awareness in mind as you review your goals and be ready to place them in your timeline!

Your mind will begin to create them!

Values Needed to Create a Money Goal

Name of Goal ....

Value	Why is it important?	Number Order

Values Needed to Create a Lifestyle Goal

Name of Goal ....

Value	Why is it important?	Number Order

Values Needed to Create a Health Goal

Name of Goal ....

Value	Why is it important?	Number Order

Designing Future Memory

Values Needed to Create a Family Goal

Name of Goal ....

Value	Why is it important?	Number Order

Values Needed to Create a Relationships Goal

Name of Goal ....

Value	Why is it important?	Number Order

Values Needed to Create a Personal Development Goal

Name of Goal ……………………………………………………..

Value	Why is it important?	Number Order

Neuro-Com Characteristics Checklist – Goal Creation

Goal for Life Area: Occupation **Goal title:**

Important Value titles			
	Value 1	Value 2	Value 3
Visual			
Self in or out of picture			
Framed or panoramic view			
Bright or dull			
Black and white or colour			
Three dimensional or flat			
Sharply focussed or blurred			
Movie or still image			
Number of pictures (if stills)			
Intensity of colour			
Feelings / kinaesthetic			
Warm, cool or cold			
Texture – rough or smooth			
Vibration – mild or intense			
Intensity of feeling			
Size			
Shape			
Weight			
Movement			
Steady or intermittent			
Internal or external			
Pressure			
Auditory			
Volume			
Pitch			
Direction			
Tone			
Rhythm			
Taste			
Smell			

Designing Future Memory

Neuro-Com Characteristics Checklist – Goal Creation

Goal for Life Area: Lifestyle **Goal title:**..

Important Value titles			
	Value 1	Value 2	Value 3
Visual			
Self in or out of picture			
Framed or panoramic view			
Bright or dull			
Black and white or colour			
Three dimensional or flat			
Sharply focussed or blurred			
Movie or still image			
Number of pictures (if stills)			
Intensity of colour			
Feelings / kinaesthetic			
Warm, cool or cold			
Texture – rough or smooth			
Vibration – mild or intense			
Intensity of feeling			
Size			
Shape			
Weight			
Movement			
Steady or intermittent			
Internal or external			
Pressure			
Auditory			
Volume			
Pitch			
Direction			
Tone			
Rhythm			
Taste			
Smell			

The Neuro-Com Program

Neuro-Com Characteristics Checklist – Goal Creation

Goal for Life Area: Family **Goal title:** ....

Important Value titles	_	_	
	Value 1	Value 2	Value 3
Visual			
Self in or out of picture			
Framed or panoramic view			
Bright or dull			
Black and white or colour			
Three dimensional or flat			
Sharply focussed or blurred			
Movie or still image			
Number of pictures (if stills)			
Intensity of colour			
Feelings / kinaesthetic			
Warm, cool or cold			
Texture – rough or smooth			
Vibration – mild or intense			
Intensity of feeling			
Size			
Shape			
Weight			
Movement			
Steady or intermittent			
Internal or external			
Pressure			
Auditory			
Volume			
Pitch			
Direction			
Tone			
Rhythm			
Taste			
Smell			

Neuro-Com Characteristics Checklist – Goal Creation

Goal for Life Area: Health **Goal title:**

Important Value titles	_	_	
	Value 1	Value 2	Value 3
Visual			
Self in or out of picture			
Framed or panoramic view			
Bright or dull			
Black and white or colour			
Three dimensional or flat			
Sharply focussed or blurred			
Movie or still image			
Number of pictures (if stills)			
Intensity of colour			
Feelings / kinaesthetic			
Warm, cool or cold			
Texture – rough or smooth			
Vibration – mild or intense			
Intensity of feeling			
Size			
Shape			
Weight			
Movement			
Steady or intermittent			
Internal or external			
Pressure			
Auditory			
Volume			
Pitch			
Direction			
Tone			
Rhythm			
Taste			
Smell			

The Neuro-Com Program

Neuro-Com Characteristics Checklist – Goal Creation

Goal for Life Area: Spiritual **Goal title:** ....

Important Value titles	–	–	
	Value 1	Value 2	Value 3
Visual			
Self in or out of picture			
Framed or panoramic view			
Bright or dull			
Black and white or colour			
Three dimensional or flat			
Sharply focussed or blurred			
Movie or still image			
Number of pictures (if stills)			
Intensity of colour			
Feelings / kinaesthetic			
Warm, cool or cold			
Texture – rough or smooth			
Vibration – mild or intense			
Intensity of feeling			
Size			
Shape			
Weight			
Movement			
Steady or intermittent			
Internal or external			
Pressure			
Auditory			
Volume			
Pitch			
Direction			
Tone			
Rhythm			
Taste			
Smell			

As you progress through these goals, you will start to see a pattern forming. When you look back at the coding methods used to create high-energy values and compare them to the values elicitation you have just completed, you will see in some cases that the coding system differs. The differences may be only minor, but the effect on the way a value is perceived can be dramatic.

For example, find a value in the forms you have just completed that is very similar to but varies slightly from a high-energy value. Perhaps the intensity of colour is less or it has a cold feel rather than warmth. It may lack a certain vibration or it may be slightly out of focus. Compare the way each value feels, and you will discover that a tiny variation can make a huge difference in the energy level in the value.

CHANGING ENERGY IN VALUES

Now that you have determined which are the important values needed to create a specific goal and have assessed them in terms of energy level verses coding, we are ready to modify the values.

For your unconscious mind to use its vast resources to create your goal, it obviously must value it highly enough to actively provide the behaviours required. We do this by defining the logical coding used in high-energy values and adjusting the coding in the required values to raise their energy.

Look back at the two Life Areas in which you spend most of your energy and review the coding used to create their highest energy value. For example, say that the Life Areas into which you put most energy are Family and Occupation, and the highest energy value you detected for Family is Love and for Occupation is Respect. Look at the coding used for each of these qualities. You will tend to find that the characteristic patterns used are nearly identical in each one.

This coding will be unique to you. I do not wish to give an example in this case, because I don't want to influence you in any way. What we do now must be on the basis of what is real for you. Fill in the form on the next page as a Master Values Design for you by copying across all the characteristics of your high-energy pattern.

The Neuro-Com Program

This form then becomes your Master Neuro-Com List. The characteristics listed here are the coding YOUR unconscious mind uses to label all emotional memories that are regarded as important to you and that are used to create high levels of activity.

This being the case, you now have a Master Plan from which to modify all the values necessary to create your new NeuroPrint or Future Plan.

Important!

It is important to remember that the way YOUR mind processes information is unique to YOU. For this reason, it is essential as you progress through these exercises that YOU do them. Do not accept advice from anyone else on what YOU SHOULD, COULD, or WOULD do to complete them. You will become accustomed to understanding how your unique unconscious program presents its belief and values systems. By becoming aware of these processes, you will be able to change any thought, feeling, or emotion at will.

Designing Future Memory

Your Master Neuro-Com Characteristics Checklist for Positive Outcomes and Emotions

Visual	
Self in or out of picture	
Framed or panoramic view	
Bright or dull	
Black and white or colour	
Three dimensional or flat	
Sharply focussed or blurred	
Movie or still image	
Number of pictures (if stills)	
Intensity of colour	
Feelings / kinaesthetic	
Warm, cool, or cold	
Texture – rough or smooth	
Vibration – mild or intense	
Intensity of feeling	
Size	
Shape	
Weight	
Movement	
Steady or intermittent	
Internal or external	
Pressure	
Auditory	
Volume	
Pitch	
Direction	
Tone	
Rhythm	
Taste	
Smell	

EXERCISE: MODIFY A LOW-LEVEL VALUE

Let's add some energy to a value that has little. Look back at the values list from one of your goals from a low-energy Life Area. For example, if Health was an area into which you put little energy, take a look at one of the goals you set for Health. Look at the coding list for the third-most important value and get a feel for the level of energy in that value. You will probably notice its energy level is low. It may appear to be just a bunch of words.

Whichever value you select follow this exact procedure:

Become aware of your friendly unconscious mind as the image or feeling you created in Chapter 4. Be aware of its presence and know it is watching and waiting for your instructions. Acknowledge that you want it to modify memory to better fulfil its highest intent for you.

With your Master Coding List in front of you, begin to consciously modify the characteristics to duplicate the style of the Master in the value on which you are working. If you have a picture, don't change the content of the picture, just the characteristics. For example if the Master is a movie and the value is a still picture, change it to a movie. Go through each characteristic and change it to match the Master coding.

When complete, check the energy content of the value and notice the higher energy. The value will seem more important!

Internally confirm with your unconscious partner that it is to lock in the change, and at the same time **clap your hands once**.

If you were careful with the exercise, you will notice that the value on which you were working now seems to have more energy and more importance. When negotiating the change with your unconscious mind, the hand-clap at the end becomes a sign-off coded instruction for your unconscious mind to log the change as permanent. It just adds a little extra energy to the deal. It's kind of like hitting the return key on a computer keyboard to signify a new paragraph.

Now go back and change all of the top three values required to create each goal so that the coding is identical to your Master Code. As you complete each goal, try to get a feel for how your mind now regards its likely outcome. Does it now feel more as if each goal can be achieved?

In this way, you can change any behaviour your mind is creating or you would like it to create. This applies equally to REMOVING behaviours you don't want, which I address in the next section.

REMOVING UNDESIRABLE BEHAVIOURS

Do you remember the exercise we did to remove a phobia? We simply changed an aspect of the presenting image or awareness. Because that situation involved a value of self-protection, we don't want to change the energy in the value, just the energy in the particular response. We negotiated with the unconscious mind to use a more appropriate behaviour while still fulfilling its highest intent of harmony and protection.

But what about removing a behaviour based on a values system that may be flawed? In this example, I choose a problem that is so prevalent that it is a major cause of anxiety in this society—money. Money being a problem stems from mixed messages we receive throughout our life. If you have a religious upbringing, the problem can sometimes be worse.

Despite the obvious need to earn money to live, a large part of our society has a conflict stemming from a values system that states that making "too much" money is bad. *He's so rich he must be a thief, or unscrupulous, or just plain dishonest.*

Your values system relating to money may be creating conflict because you have two or more separate value systems working at the same time. This creates a classic values conflict that we discussed in Chapter 5. You could use the Parts Integration process we discussed, or you could choose to look at the underlying values and modify the energy in them.

Select a value relating to money that creates a values conflict. Let's say you discover a very strong positive value related to achieving wealth—unmitigated screaming riches. The ability to live in a style most will only dream of is a very strong force. Such a force drives the world economy and keeps everything moving.

On the other hand is the value that says you should not crave wealth. If you do not believe you have that value embedded in your system, let me ask you a question: Are you wealthy?

If not, the value can only come from two areas: either you have not given your mind an instruction to create wealth, or you have a block. This one is close to my heart. When I was very young, I decided to retire at the age of 39 as a millionaire. I succeeded but apparently still had a block about feeling as if I deserved it. My accountant stole the lot within a year and a half!

Become aware of your unconscious mind and request a view of all values related to wealth. You may become aware of several values and their associated images / feelings. See if there is one that feels strongly that either wealth is not good for the soul or that you do not deserve it. If the feeling is strong you may notice that it presents to you with similar coding to your Master Code. Am I correct?

If you wish to create wealth, you need to defuse this value. Simply change some of the coding so that it becomes less energetic coding. If the value is coded as a movie, change it to a still picture and bring it out in front of you as if you are looking at a postcard. If it feels hard, soften it; if it is colourful, turn it to black and white. As you alter these things, you will notice the energy drifts out of the view. Seal the changes with a clap to instruct the unconscious mind to store the changes in memory.

Now you might like to go back to the part of you that wants to create wealth and feel how much stronger it is. In this way, you can change the values balance to create anything you consciously desire.

A LIFE-CHANGING UNDERSTANDING

Always remember: *It is the conscious mind that is the controller. Your unconscious mind is the servant and will always respond to instructions given in a language that it can understand—Neuro-Com.*

CHAPTER EIGHT

Creating Happiness

> **This module will discuss:**
>
> - Balancing success with personal happiness
> - What makes happiness a reality
> - What stops most people from being happy
> - The highest intent of your mind
> - Neuro-Com and Relationships
> - Neuro-Com and religious thought

BALANCING SUCCESS WITH PERSONAL HAPPINESS

This short section acts as a **warning** to all who pass this way.

As we have progressed through this program, and you have become aware of your potential to create any outcome you wish, there is a risk that you will narrow your use of the skills to only one area of your life. While I have tried to ensure that there is balance in your NeuroPrint for the future, some readers will not take heed.

The strategies you have learned are very powerful for creating change and providing control over how your mind performs for you. If you have followed through on all the exercises, you will already be noticing the difference in the way your life is evolving. Certainly others will be noticing a difference in your behaviours.

You may be tempted to use these new skills to focus on developing the trappings of success and wealth. For most of us, that area of life has a strong emotional pull. If you head down that path, please make sure that you create balance in your life at the same time.

Your mind is capable of working on many strategies at once behind the scenes. It is very efficient in what it does. Let it use that immense capability to provide the trappings you desire, but also to give you choices surrounding your relationships, friends, and personal well-being. Stories of wealthy people living a miserable life abound in literature and in reality. Heed the old saying: "There is little point in gaining the world if in doing so you lose your soul."

Happiness can come from a million sources, but it is only available to us right now, in this moment. To be happy is a choice. We either decide to make that choice or not, and we may never get the chance again to enjoy the feelings that are happiness if we don't choose it now. I use the NOW a lot because NOW is the only reality we have. I will discuss the more spiritual aspects of NOW a little later for those of you who wish to understand a little more about yourself and the overlying reality of the mind. For now, I'll discuss some elements of using Neuro-Com to balance your life.

WHAT MAKES HAPPINESS A REALITY?

Happiness is simply a NeuroDynamic state in which your unconscious mind produces, at certain times, a mix of kinaesthetic strategies that make you feel good. The ultimate awareness is produced by a series of neurotransmitters throughout the body in response to a conscious decision or an unconscious reaction to an environment or events. The prime neurotransmitters are a group called endorphins, but Serotonin and Dopamine also have a role in creating such an awareness

Most of us have experienced happiness at some time or other. We have a vague awareness of what it feels like but usually depend on external sources to trigger the emotion. How would you like to be able to trigger it at a moment's notice? How would you like to enjoy happiness as a normal way of life? In this chapter, we will look at two components:

- Internal happiness—our relationship with ourselves
- External influences—our relationships with others

Both components of creating happiness involve using your skills in Neuro-Com to define what coding your mind uses to trigger happy feelings.

Most of what we have covered in this program revolves around using Neuro-Com strategies to remove unwanted emotional interference and modifying values to create a different future. Now let's look at using them to create or enhance an emotion.

WHAT STOPS MOST PEOPLE FROM BEING HAPPY?

The answer to this question should now be obvious with your understanding of how the unconscious mind creates emotional responses from past memory. We also have a tendency to create expectations of what should happen in our life, often based on false information, and then compare reality with our expectations. If we are not totally in control of our environment, we are often disappointed.

Does this mean that we should crawl back under a log and have no expectations? Absolutely not! What it does mean, however, is that we have to look at ways to modify our reaction to our environment and the way we expect others to behave.

As with all emotional reactions, we control our level of happiness, right now, in this moment. By learning to live in this moment emotional memory chatter is going on in the background to create the feeling we relate to as "unhappiness." If you have been through all the exercises in this program, you already know how to change an emotion simply by changing the characteristics of the emotion. By being conscious of what we are doing and how we are reacting on a moment-by-moment basis, we control our environment.

What I mean by that is that if you are washing the car, wash the car. If you are eating a meal, eat the meal. If you are talking to someone, listen to them and talk. If you are making love, make love. In other words, concentrate on what you are doing in the moment without reflecting on the past or projecting into the future. The future will take care of itself and will be created based on how you have programmed it during these exercises.

I must clarify something here in case what you just read is confusing. Some will think I have just said you should not think about the future and may ask, "So how can I plan my future?" That is not what I said. When you are planning your future and creating your NeuroPrint during this program, you are actually working in the NOW. Yes, you are dealing with the values characteristics required to make things work, but that is simply a process you are using in the moment. You are going through the process NOW. Once the NeuroPrint is in place, your unconscious mind will create it automatically, and you won't need to think about it again. You can go back to concentrating on what is happening NOW.

The only thing that stops us from being happy is our tendency to live our lives in past memories and emotional reactions and the future projections and the fears they create. For instance you can be drinking a cup of coffee but not tasting it. You don't have any awareness of the feel of the mug, or its temperature, unless it is so hot it burns you. You don't feel the liquid on your lips and you take no notice of the exquisite aroma of the coffee. You drink the coffee but you are generally thinking about a dozen other things and feeling the emotions of the past and anxieties driven by your perception of the future.

I often have people say to me that they live in now, but then talk about why things are not right or they are concerned about the future. Living in NOW for them is not day dreaming about the future or constantly remembering the past. What they don't understand is that their day to day reactions and conversations are filled with the decisions and emotions of the past memory bank. They do not experience the wonders of what is happening right in front of them. They are living in anticipation of the next event.

We often live in anticipation of something going wrong. We spend a great part of our lives working to bring home sufficient money to survive and create a lifestyle. We forget that we don't have a lifestyle to enjoy because it's always somewhere in the future. We destroy our relationships by creating expectations of others and ignore the warmth and physical comfort that can be derived from them NOW.

We strive to accumulate physical possessions to impress family and friends—and even strangers—we encounter every day so that our lousy self-image can get a boost. Instead, we should be dealing with our self-image problems in the first place.

THE HIGHEST INTENT OF YOUR MIND

I know your unconscious mind is watching and absorbing this information as you read it. It is processing it faster than you are consciously aware and comparing it to what it has recorded as a viable knowledge or program. It is comparing its message as to whether it conforms to its highest intent.

We have already discussed why your unconscious soul memory does what it does for you. Its role is to protect you from extinction and create emotional balance in your life. Its role is to provide harmony. Unfortunately, its definition of protection and harmony often doesn't match the logical definition, causing you to believe that it is trying to deliberately harm you. It is not. It is just doing what it has been programmed to do.

Earlier in the program, we engaged in an exercise to make friends with a representation of your unconscious mind. In deciding to create happiness in this life, it is important that you always treat your unconscious memory as a friend. Become proficient in the Neuro-Com techniques you have learned in this program, and you will always be able to ask your unconscious for what you want and be in control of how you feel. The more you control interactions with your unconscious, the more it will accept your decisions and provide the emotional and behavioural environment you desire.

The Neuro-Com Program

NEURO-COM IN RELATIONSHIPS—DOING IT WITH OTHERS!

The way people interact occupies a great deal of time for the average human. The way we interact with others determines a great deal of our happiness or dissatisfaction. Our relationships with friends, family, lovers, workmates, and others close to us ultimately determine our successes and failures in almost everything we do. They also dramatically affect stress levels and resultant health issues. It is thus important that we spend time and energy to try to get them in balance and harmony.

Our self-image, values, attitudes, and resultant behaviours all derive from the program we took on during that first critical five years of our life, including the thought-feeling reactions engendered in the uterus. We take on embedded memories of what relationships are about, many of which are based on invalid information. We then tend to carry those values and the resultant attitudes and behaviours forward into our own relationships. As such, we very often duplicate the relationships of our parents, whether good or bad.

"THE PROBLEM WITH RELATIONSHIPS IS......"

We have already seen how the unconscious soul memory organises itself into emotional and content groups. Over time, memory groupings developed while we are in a state of waking hypnosis during our earliest five years and evolved into a large variety of complex NeuroDynamic reactive groups, many of which remain in conflict with one another.

For example, let's look at how the cause of a major portion of stress-inducing behaviours develops via self-image conflict. It is unfortunate that the human race has evolved to hold a relatively negative view of itself. We tend to reflect this through criticising other people, events, and circumstances. During that first five years, we don't have the ability to rationalise what is going on around us, so we absorb the comments and attitudes of those around us, taking them on as fact.

We rarely encourage our children. Instead, more often than not, we tell them directly they are doing the wrong thing, or say things such as "don't be stupid" or "you should try harder." The inference is often that they are not good enough as they are or should endeavour to be better. The result is that the vast majority of the human race has a terrible self-image.

So, we have established that self-image is of real concern to most of us. As you know, this can be resolved readily. Where it really presents us with an issue, however, is when another memory group conflicts with our general self-image group. As we evolve, there are almost always times we feel good about ourselves. It may be an event, a comment, or even a hug from a smiling relative that opens our "positive image" account at the memory bank. Over time, this new memory series, complete with warm and fuzzy feelings, develops into a group with sufficient emotional content to present to consciousness as a thought-feeling reaction when self-image is accessed.

Now we have a conflict. Self-image is accessed, and the thought-feeling reaction produces two different scenarios to consciousness at the same time. One tells you that you are okay and the other says you aren't. Most of us do not stop to evaluate what's going on and allow the stronger of the two emotional groups to create the behaviour that follows. But there is always that ever-present conflict that you can't put your finger on.

But, you know it's there. That unconscious battle creates serious trauma; in the hundreds of more serious cases I've encountered, they almost always end up creating health problems and self-destructive behaviour.

The same internal value conflicts can occur in almost every area of life. Conflicting beliefs and values are disturbing enough within our own mind. Where they really create havoc is in relationships, because we now not only have internal conflicts with ourselves, but we have two individual memories interacting! Each has its own beliefs, values, and attitudes that are always visible to the other party through language and touch and through the more subliminal communications of skin colour, eye contact, pupil dilation, behaviour, and voice tone. Any awareness of differences of thought or feeling have the potential to create disharmony in a relationship, whether or not either party is consciously aware of the conflict!

Very often when we meet another person and click it is because our unconscious recognises patterns that it has stored as desirable. This can come from behaviours or recognition of similar learning or interests. We have come to that point because we are on a life path that has brought us there.

Unfortunately, we don't stay at that point in time forever. We move off in the same direction we were going. Values change, learning becomes different and behaviour changes over time based on the program we are carrying. The person we met and were so attracted to is also on a path—his or her own. As time passes, the distance between us often grows wider. Our unconscious minds no longer recognise the other in the same way, so we gradually grow apart again. Conflicts begin because we now have different views of the world. Evolution has taken its course.

My experience clinically has found that the areas that create most conflict with relationships are sex, money, religion, and lack of respect for the other's views. These occur as the partners move apart until we eventually start looking for points to argue.

It's no wonder the statistics on long-term relationships are so dismal!

EXPECTATIONS

We all expect different things from our interaction with others. What we expect is based on the belief and values system we have taken on, which are based on the relationships in which we saw those in authority engaging when we were kids. Our unconscious memory continues to base our attitudes and consequent behaviours toward others on those embedded values.

When we meet someone, our unconscious mind evaluates that person in light of his or her behaviour, both physical and verbal, conscious and unconscious. It watches for inconsistencies with eye contact, pupil dilation, movement, smell, and other behaviours. If the thought-feeling reaction is comfortable, we establish communication. If not, we walk away. If the reaction is strongly positive, we pursue the association. And of all this is processed and determined in a fraction of a second.

As we spend time with that person, the initial emotional reaction is overlaid with other expectations we place on the relationship with them. We are now trying to have a completely different soul memory, with a completely different program and values, fit inside our program. Where the beliefs and values are at serious odds, this scenario usually doesn't work and causes conflict similar to our internal values conflicts, which we have already discussed.

So what is the answer to resolving these issues? If you are having problems or you are not completely comfortable in a relationship of any sort, you first need to look at the expectations you are placing on the other party. Have you become involved with someone who is like one of your parents? Look at the relationship you have and find out why you are in it. Is it in balance, with both of you giving and receiving? Are you trying to put the relationship in a pigeonhole that it shouldn't be in?

A relationship can be anything from an enemy to a loving marriage. Between those extremes is infinite variety, but we tend to follow social rules of putting it into a category such as friendship, very good friendship, sexual, committed partnership, and marriage. Often, trying to work within these parameters puts stress on an otherwise wonderful association. Your relationship with the person with whom you are engaging is UNIQUE. It involves two minds that are unique. It should be regarded as such and lived without labels, whether it fits within social labels or not.

It will only work if you both give it permission to be fluid, to enjoy its fluidity in the moment. If you like, give your relationship a new label, exclusive to you—a "soulaship"—or some other label with no meaning except to you as a pair! In that way, you can take out some of the expectations society places on you and allow yourselves to negotiate a set of rules with which you are both comfortable.

Try backing away and getting a clear view on what you are feeling. If something doesn't feel right, then see if the feeling is legitimate **for this relationship**. Remember, you may be overlaying past relationships or parental relationships on a situation that is much better. The result of allowing such an overlay will always degrade the pleasure you could be getting with the person with whom you are now involved.

What gives you pleasure in this relationship? Is it the feeling of elevated self-worth, trust, mutual respect, love, sex, or making love (they are vastly different!) There is nothing more wonderful in human life than being totally aware of the feeling of a gentle, caring touch or the warmth of feeling truly loved. The only way to really enjoy such pleasures and honour them completely is to experience them in NOW.

You cannot and should not try to live a relationship for the future. Only NOW can be lived in consciousness. The past and its projected future are the realms of an unconscious program that is often based on inaccuracies and false expectations.

By living in this moment you can enjoy the physical, mental, and emotional aspects of a mutual closeness that is special and can never be lived again. Living NOW has no thought-feeling reactions to disturb the beauty and freedom of the moment. And, a wonderful side effect of the decision to live an unlabelled relationship in NOW is that there is nothing to prevent that feeling from existing in every NOW forever. NOW never ends!!!!

You may also need to look at your value systems in relation to the situation. If you communicate with the person and take a look at the directions your lives are taking, you may find that your natural direction is now no longer going in the same way as the other person's. Look at creating some common goals and work through the process outlined in Chapters 6 and 7 to create some congruency between you.

THE FIRST STEP TO NOW

We have already discussed the need to monitor the thought-feeling reactions from the unconscious memory. A thousand times per minute, your unconscious memory is accessed to determine if there are any past recorded responses to the current situation, conversation, or event. In milliseconds, you are presented with a response to use that has worked before that allows the relevant part of the mind to fulfil its function, that is, to protect you. Rather than reacting to the response your mind gives you, decide if you want the response and discard it if not.

You can only do this in NOW and by being aware of the responses being presented. Once the response has been processed and the behaviour implemented, it is too late—you have already added to the emotional gestalt that created the response in the first place. By watching the thought-feeling reaction and responding consciously in a different way to the expected response, the part of the mind that created it is joined to a new behaviour. When sufficient energy is placed in the new behavioural response, it will become the prime thought-feeling reaction in future.

By doing this on a consistent basis, the types of thought-feeling reactions with which you are presented become consistent with valid input rather than protecting an invalid past. This allows you to enjoy life by living in this moment, in NOW.

Old psychology and psychiatric techniques try to do this by evoking the thought-feeling reaction and changing the emotional energy and behaviour over a long period of time. Using the NeuroDynamic techniques we have discussed allows you to eliminate the old though-feeling reaction very quickly, replacing it with the desired behaviours.

A major part of the process is to eliminate the internal gestalt conflicts that cause so much stress and self-doubt. Typical responses to such conflicts involve confusion, fear with no apparent cause, anger, and eventually, biochemical imbalances and psychosis. I have dealt with many, many people, both male and female, who had spent years in the offices of psychologists and psychiatrists trying to cope with this problem. Integrating the parts of the mind that create the problem is really a simple matter. In many cases, it can take as little as an hour to remove a lifelong trauma, completely and permanently. Even horrifying phobias can be permanently removed within minutes!

The procedure is simple. By understanding the process **your** unconscious mind uses to communicate with you, you can negotiate a truce and then integrate the parts of the mind involved. Each part has its own personality, although it is not conscious of itself. It is purely reactive to the environment. When it is shown that its current behaviours are not fulfilling its highest intent for you, it will drop its behaviour very quickly, *provided it is given permission to access other, more suitable and protective behaviours to replace the discarded ones.*

Be gentle with your mind. You may think it is trying to play tricks on you, hurt you, or even destroy you. It is important to understand that no matter how aggressive a part seems to be, and how much damage it creates in your life, it is actually trying to protect you. It has just taken on a group of behaviours that it believes will stop you from being physically hurt, even when the biological results are just as damaging. It is purely reacting to an event or circumstance as it has been told to do.

When you identify the parts of the unconscious that are creating a conflict internally (a Parts Conflict), no matter what belief system or value they relate to, each is typically unaware of the other's existence! Each produces a thought-feeling reaction based on the program that memory group is running at the time. But when they are introduced to each other in their own language and a truce and integration is negotiated, watch the amazing, life-transforming results!

In a relationship, by first removing the inhibiting personal internal conflicts, you can then communicate with the other person in your life clearly and without ambiguity. You can listen with an open mind and stop yourself from reacting to information or behaviour you would normally have found irritating. Whether you like it or not, everyone has a right to their own belief system, values, and philosophy of life. We have no right to challenge that unless the resultant behaviours create harm for others.

COMMUNICATION IN RELATIONSHIPS

If your relationships are important to you (I believe they should be), you need to learn to communicate openly and honestly if you want them to survive. Each of you must give and receive in a relationship for it to work. It's not as easy as it sounds for most of us, because our unconscious program tries to protect us from conflict and trauma. We often view verbal communication as being a creator of conflict.

Just as you need to be willing to communicate your needs, fears, anxieties, and desires to your partner, you must also LISTEN and respond to them. Too often we get so involved in our day-to-day lives that we substitute "busy" behaviour to avoid getting into uncomfortable space with our partners. I know. I have been guilty of this in the past, at great pain and cost to both. We think that avoiding a discussion of our emotional issues will make the problems go away, but it doesn't. Usually, the issues turn from something easily fixed into a major hurdle. One negative behaviour leads to another, until the differences between you outweigh the love or affection you used to have. You end up destroying something that is precious and rare.

Be careful of what you convey through your behaviour and tone of voice. Our unconscious mind has a vast store of information relating to even the most minor hand movement, eye movement, or changes in skin colour and pupil dilation. A tiny change in voice tone or speech rate communicates a great deal to another mind. If your language and behaviour don't match at a subliminal level, that is, below the level of conscious awareness, disharmony will result. This ultimately affects trust and deteriorates the intensity of positive feelings. If the conflict between what you say and do is consistent over a long period, you can almost guarantee the relationship won't last. The moral of the story is to be honest with your partner.

THE FOUNDATIONS OF HUMANITY

If you gain nothing else from this program I implore you to learn and teach three important principals, on the back of which is carried the future of humanity:

First, treat yourself and everyone in your life as an individual. Respect where they have come from and that some behaviours you may find distasteful come from programs over which they've had little control. Be gentle in your judgements, for they also will judge you. Try to avoid placing people in boxes. I know many people judge their friends and acquaintances by their star signs, religion, nationality, shape of their body or face, the way they dress, education, or other more esoteric rituals. While most people fit into one sort of group or another, within such loose groupings is an infinite variety. Treat everyone as an individual, worthy of being valued and honoured. If you can't respect someone for who they are, don't become involved in their life.

Second, learn the skills of communication so that you can work through issues and differences between you. If you don't, you will destroy a precious friendship or become disillusioned with love. The pain from a broken relationship is intense. Often, it causes so much distress that it results in the death of the individual, through disease or suicide. The discomfort of learning to expose your vulnerability through communication will give you a wonderful sense of freedom and joy. By being honest in your communications, you create congruency. By allowing yourself to use touch and tone of voice to convey warmth, you also get the rewards and pleasures of intimacy. Convey affection through an appropriate hug or respect through a warm handshake.

Third, learn the Principle of **Edification** and practice it every moment of your life. It is one of the most important keys to the development of the human race and its future survival. Put simply, it means to "build up, to enhance". In the context of relationships with other human beings, it simply means to look for the good in others and let them know you appreciate them for who they are and their choices in life. In reality, there is no good or bad, and we tend to judge people on our own failings and dislikes. Such judgement is arrogant and unnecessary. By edifying everyone that comes into your life, by finding the good and praising it, you let that person feel good about him- or herself, and, in turn, they will feel good about you. If you have trouble finding anything good about a person's personality, skills, or accomplishments, praise the way they clean their shoes! Just avoid pulling people down. In a close relationship, edification becomes the cornerstone for respect, love, and longevity. Its practice can make you rich in every way.

WHY ARE RELATIONSHIPS SO IMPORTANT?

The human race has been misled. Generation after generation has gone down the path of self-gratification, physical reality, and accumulating assets. We have strayed from caring for and looking after others as carefully as we do ourselves. Relationships between people, between groups, and between nations are degrading at an alarming rate. Lack of mutual communication and edification is isolating individuals, creating anger and frustration. The individual is becoming an island.

Unless we take responsibility for others as well as ourselves, we stand to lose everything. There are many exponents of metaphysics and alternate views of personal development that will tell you that you are only responsible for yourself—that others create their own environment and should therefore wear the results of what you do to them. We are all part of one energy and one mind. We as individuals and as a soul memory are simply a part of that mind, just as reactive as a separate memory group within our own unconscious. To say we can operate in isolation is stupidity and exhibits no personal experience of the reality of NOW. Every individual that comes into our lives is part of us just as we are part of them.

We are connected in energy no matter what the distance between us. We all contribute to the collective unconscious and are responsible for what we feed back to it. Every memory and emotional gestalt we claim as our own soul also belongs to the collective unconscious. Everyone around us, near or far, recognises and is reacted on by our fears, angers, loves, and passions. As we lose the ability to love, as we allow anger and disharmony to increase, we add to the millions of others doing the same to the group, national, and global memory. When the masses of negative emotions stored have greater energy than the emotions of love and acceptance, the human race has always gone to war to try to create balance.

We are all responsible for each other. Our relationships with those around us will determine our survival on this plane.

THE NEURODYNAMICS OF RELATIONSHIPS

Think about all the people you know. How many of them are in great relationships? How many times have you become part of a conversation that discusses the impending break-up of a marriage or one that has just occurred and surprised everyone?

Look at the facts. In the Western world, 50% of first marriages break up. Sixty per cent of second marriages also hit the rocks and sink. Lives are destroyed, anger is rampant, and the lawyers make a fortune. In looking at the real facts of relationships, it gets worse. I have seen and studied thousands of relationships, marriages, defactos, and friendships. Here are the statistics.

Of 1,000 relationships of any kind:

500 will dissolve the partnership

400 will stay in the relationship and tolerate the differences between the partners. They may stay together because of children or for reasons of security. Generally, the players are not really happy and may feel friendship or less. The players are highly likely to have one or more affairs, which are never discussed or brought out into the open.

90 will be in relationships that are relatively stable and could be regarded as good to great friendships. Traumas are minimised. The relationship may occasionally be made more stable by a minor fling on the side, secretly of course!

10 out of the 1,000, or just 1%, have a long, happy, and loving relationship. These are the people you see, at 60 years old, walking down the street, hand-in-hand. Only one per cent!

And, if you want to explore the elusive soul partnership, less than 0.1% can achieve the exquisite perfection of this much sought after rarity. This society tries to sell the idea of marriage being the perfect means to a happy life. The religions, and therefore the lawmakers, have effectively placed a huge guilt trip on us by indicating that the only acceptable sexual relationship occurs within marriage. The only way to have a long-term, loving bond is within a permanent, flexible structure.

The very nature of the human mind and energetic memory system makes the so-called "perfect" relationship a practical impossibility, unless there is work done on the individuals' value system and life focus. We all have a unique memory structure based on the individual's entire recorded personal history. Everyone else has a different recording. As we have already discussed, this means that each of us has a different values system and resultant attitudes and behaviours. These combine to head us in a certain general direction in life and allow us to develop various skills and desires.

We believe that the world should be a certain way and that people should act a certain way. When they don't, we get upset, uncomfortable, or angry. Our permanent, loving, and perfect partner also has a recorded belief and value system that is highly unlikely to be anything like yours! He or she has lived a different life. They have different parents and different grandparents. They may have gone to different schools and, in most cases, are a different sex. Just the difference in sex and the social program of being male or female means the thinking style of your partner is likely to differ. They have a specific program that will draw them into a specific lifestyle and direction in life. Their rate and style of emotional evolution is almost certain to be different to your program.

We are usually attracted to someone, sexually or otherwise, by the fact that our unconscious mind recognises certain characteristics to which it relates. The characteristics will be those that your mind recognises as being suitable for a relationship. As you already know, that view of a relationship is likely to revolve around your energetic memory of your parent's relationship! So, if your parent's relationship was not made in heaven, the chances are that your program will draw you into a relationship that is less than perfect!

The Neuro-Com Program

Recognition gap becomes wider over time

Two unconscious minds "recognise each other as being similar at this point in time = attraction

Life direction path determined by unconscious

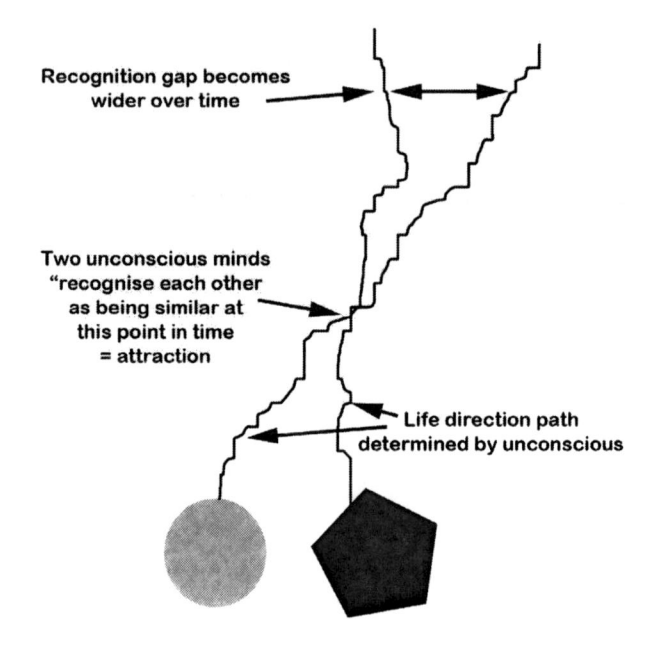

Figure 10. The creation and destruction of relationships

Because the statistics show your parents had a 50% chance of breaking up and a further 40% chance of being in turmoil, the odds against you finding the right partner for a permanent relationship are terrible!

Add to this that our on-going emotional evolution will continue to send us in a predetermined direction, and it is likely that whatever positive aspects of attraction you were consciously aware of will not survive. If you originally thought you had a lot in common, three or four years down the track, you may see a totally different view.

To explain this a more clearly, let's say that your emotional evolution can be gauged by a Life Direction Pattern (LDP). Depending on our program, each of us has our own unique pattern. We are attracted to individuals depending on how closely our LDPs match at the time of initial contact. How long we stay in tune will be determined by how long our LDPs remain within a critical energy threshold. When the energy drops below the critical level, our unconscious program is no longer recognising a useful input and will lead you off in a new search. To maintain a long-term match in LDPs, we need to do some work on our basic program.

The near-to-perfect relationship is possible, if you want it. But you must be prepared to use some NeuroDynamic techniques on your own program and preferably involve your ideal partner. By modifying your LDPs so that they have some common direction, you can create whatever relationship you want, for as long as you want it!

THE IDEAL RELATIONSHIP

Now we can view a relationship in terms of the joint values that we have, whether they are positive or negative. Remember, a value is simply a belief system that holds significant emotional energy. It is our values that tend to drive our behaviours, including the way we think, walk, and talk. They make us attracted or repelled by people, events, and places in our lives.

Knowing this, we can develop an appropriate working model for the ideal relationship.

A relationship actually creates a third entity that involves part or all of our belief and values systems. To show this graphically let's look at an average relationship.

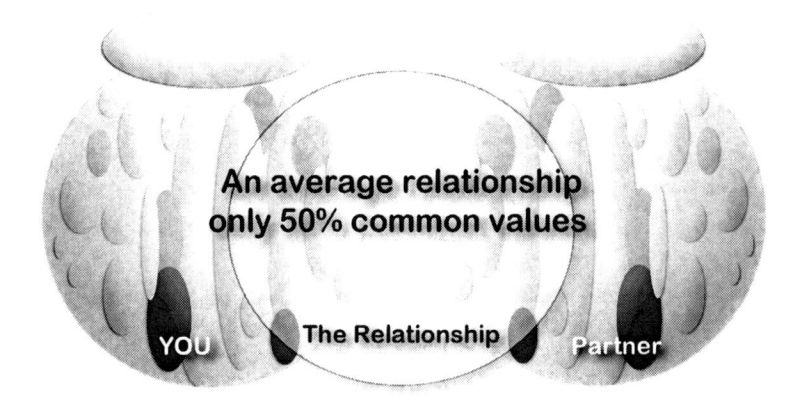

Figure 11. An Average Relationship

In a true, loving relationship, love requires three things to support it and on which it can build.

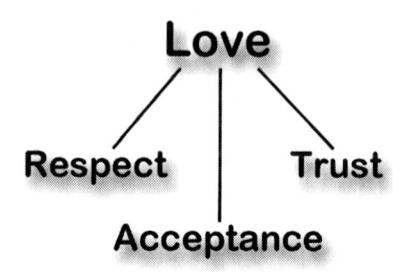

```
            Love
           / | \
          /  |  \
    Respect  |  Trust
             |
        Acceptance
```

Figure 12. The essential components of good relationships

The trust and respect are self-explanatory. They foster a sense of safety, security, and longevity. Trust and respect are primarily driven by the joint values that each party to the relationship shares, that is, inside the relationship circle shown above.

Acceptance is another matter. Acceptance involves the ability of one partner to accept the beliefs and values (and hence the behaviours) of the partner that fall outside the circle of common values. In other words, it's those parts of your partner's personality that may make you grind your teeth, clench your fist, or cringe in disbelief. But there is a catch. The pool of acceptance is limited and has a drain tap in the bottom of its reservoir. Every time you partner does something that annoys you or is totally outside your value system, it drains a little of this precious acceptance from your reservoir. And, when your supply of acceptance is getting close to exhausted by what you perceive as bad behaviour, respect begins to deplete. When respect is nearly gone, trust also begins to deplete. Eventually, there is not sufficient respect or trust to sustain LOVE, and it dies also. The relationship has ended and is often irretrievable.

This is so sad, especially when LOVE is such a rare and priceless commodity. We allow it to drain away and die because we cannot accept the behaviours of a partner in a relationship that usually starts with such promise.

The fewer values we have in common, the more of our behaviours lie outside the relationship circle. In such cases, acceptance is drained very quickly and the relationship dies a rapid death, but not always without pain. The following represents a relationship that is doomed before it begins. In this example the common values inside the relationship circle comprise only a small part of each individual's total values.

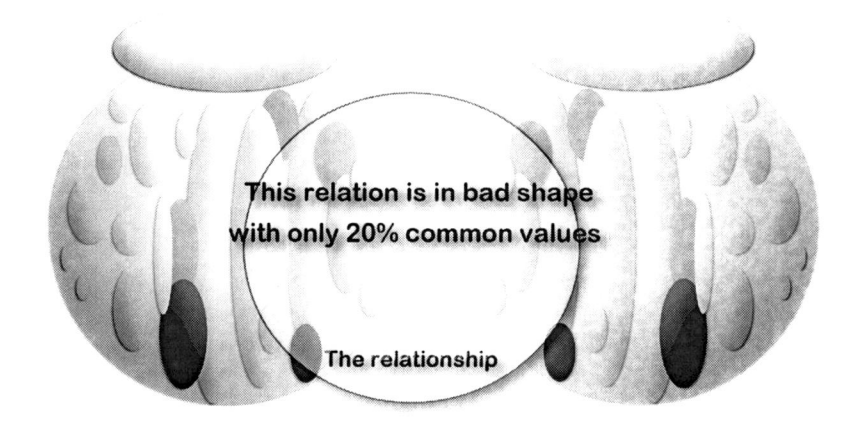

Figure 13. This Relationship is in Crisis

In this scenario, the relationship circle incorporates few joint values, and thus requires a high degree of acceptance to cater to all the values that are not included. In this case, the two people effectively place a high value on individuality, and the relationship would be, at best, a struggle.

In the ideal relationship, you select a partner with a high degree of common values related to life's major concerns, with far fewer beliefs and values falling outside the relationship circle. Such a relationship can last a long time, if not forever, because the drain on acceptance is always small. Trust and respect remain high, and living under the same roof becomes easy.

The Neuro-Com Program

This relation is in good shape with 80% common values

The Relationship

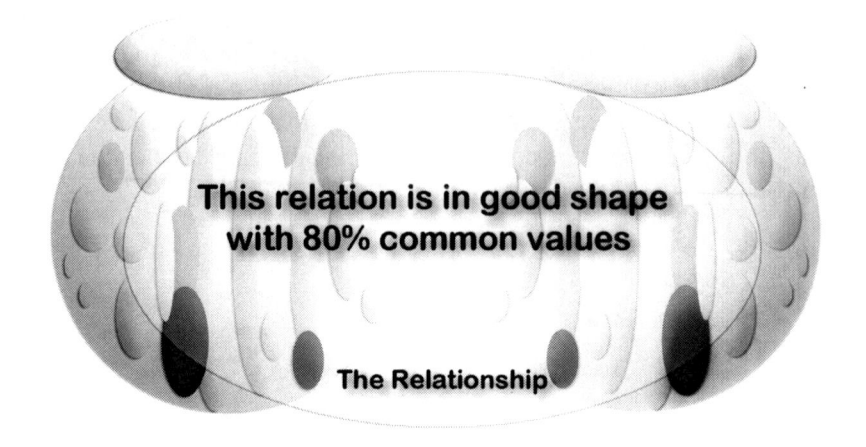

Figure 14. A great balanced relationship

THE ELUSIVE SOUL PARTNERSHIP

We often hear of the wonderful utopia of soul partnerships, in which a couple is so well matched that nothing comes between them. Love is experienced as a deep, almost spiritual experience. Being in such a relationship seems like heaven on earth with an amazing feeling of security, safety, and a permanence that feels comfortable. Such relationships are often healing, growing, and passionate. They are the envy of most, but many people do not believe they exist.

But they do. My estimate is that they occur in less than one-tenth of one per cent of relationships. Now that doesn't seem like a lot, and for the most part they happen by chance. So what is it? Can it be created?

Using the same model we have implemented above, a soul relationship is one in which the belief and value systems of both partners are almost identical, certainly among the major values. A Soul relationship looks like this the illustration below.

> This "soul" relation is in great shape with 95% common values
>
> The relationship

Figure 15. The Elusive SOUL Relationship

So, we must ask ourselves: can such a perfect relationship be created?

Well, yes. And no. No because many people (dare I say most?) are self-oriented and consequently see and interact with the world in light of how it affects them. Other people are expected to conform to their demands or unconscious perceptions. Such people rarely create any kind of long-term relationship and are a major proportion of the 55% of failed relationships.

However the yes comes from the fact that provided both parties have a deep desire to create the perfect relationship, and are willing to do the work, it is possible to negotiate a centre point on beliefs and values. Using Neuro-Com principles, you can reprogram conflicting beliefs and values to come close to, if not fully achieve, a soul relationship.

If you wish to try, go through the exercises that follow—both of you. Explore the values you identify and see the commonalities and differences between you. At the end of this document I have included an additional questionnaire that I have used in fixing damaged relationships. Go through that and identify the commonalities and differences between you. This can then act as a template for honest and open discussion and a commitment to change things that conflict.

WARNING! Tread these paths gently and with compassion! Sometimes such an exercise becomes confrontational and needs an informed mediator familiar with Neuro-Com principles. Sometimes the differences become so glaring that it triggers a decision to part company. But at least you know; at least your discussion can be more open and penetrating. If you find you cannot come to a common resolution of beliefs and values, then you have a basis for a decision whether to stay or go. Perhaps there is someone out there who matches your values more closely. Or, perhaps it is worth taking a good look at the conflicting values, drop the ego, and change for the sake of a better relationship.

Remember: YOU HAVE BEEN WARNED. You need to be both absolutely committed to creating a solid, values based relationship and mutual commitment before you attempt this exercise. It is very revealing and for some may be confronting.

Establishing Your Relationship Values

In establishing and continuing the relationship, it is important to understand the belief and value system of the other party.

Both parties to a relationship should complete the following survey. It is important that you spend sufficient time with this exercise and be completely honest about your answers. Each of you should complete your own survey without discussing it or referring to your partner and his or her answers. The discussion around variations in your beliefs in your value system will come later. **Do not answer these questions on the basis of how you think your partner or your councillor would wish to hear them.**

Your name _____

Date this form is being completed _____

How long have you been in this relationship? _____

What would you like to achieve by taking part in this process?

_____

_____

Love can be interpreted in many ways. It is different, or at least perceived to be different, depending on the circumstance in which it is experienced. For example, the love you have for a child differs from the love you have for a close friend, which in turn differs from the love one has for a life partner.

Do you believe you love your existing partner? _____

What type of love do you believe that it is? Is it the love you would have for a close friend, or is it the love you might have for a lover or soul mate?

_____

Do you think that your partner loves you? If so, what type of love do you think he or she has for you?

_____

Do you believe you can change the way we your partner thinks, acts, or feels?

_____

When faced with day-to-day activities or a new situation, do you consider the thoughts and feelings of your partner as part of a decision-making process?

___

In your day-to-day life, do you view the world and other people on the basis of how they affect **you**, your life, your needs, and your desires?

___

Do you think your partner considers your needs and desires as part of his or her decision-making process?

___

How important are physical attributes in your perception of your partner?

___

Describe the physical attributes that you would like your ideal partner to have.

___

___

___

___

___

Does your partner have these attributes?

_____

If not, what do you think they are lacking?

_____

_____

_____

What are the **major** things that you dislike about your partner?

_____

_____

_____

_____

_____

What other **minor** things do you dislike about your partner? These are the things that sometimes irritate you, but you may not say anything to your partner about them. For example, perhaps your partner is messy around the house, just leaving towels where they shouldn't be. Perhaps it is something about how they speak to you that annoys you. Think of as many minor issues as you can, because it is these minor issues that are usually the things that will destroy the relationship.

_____

_____

(Use additional sheets or your journal to answer this question if there is insufficient room here!)

Which of your behaviours do you think would annoy your partner?

What are the **major** factors that you **like** about your partner?

Creating Happiness

What are the **small** things that you really like about your partner that makes you feel good about you and your relationship?

_____

_____

_____

_____

_____

_____

Three of the major issues in destructive relationships include sex, money, and communications or lack of communications. Sex is an issue that looms large in the minds of most people. In many ways, it drives our existence, as it perhaps should in the natural environment. However, in our society and in our artificial environment, sex often becomes a major issue in relationships because of different beliefs and values surrounding the subject. Men demand different things from sex than women do.

The following questions, as always, should be treated as totally confidential and private. I suggest that you do not discuss your answers to these questions yet with your partner until both of you have completed the questions. Answer them honestly as though no one else will ever read them. In other words, be completely honest with yourself. Feel free to elaborate with additional comments as you wish.

Are you totally comfortable discussing sex with other people?

_____

Are you totally comfortable discussing your personal sex life with your partner?

Do you enjoy your current sexual experience with your partner all the time?

Do you think that your sex life is satisfactory and fulfilling?

Do you have fantasies of a sex life outside your existing relationship?

What aspects of another person are important to you in creating sexual desire?

Does your partner create a desire in you to have sex?

Do you differentiate between having sex and making love? If so, in what way?

Do you think sex is important to your partner? If not, why do you think this is the case?

Do you fulfil your own needs before those of your partner?

Do you think your partner is happy with your current sex life?

Is there anything missing from your existing relationship that your ideal relationship may contain from a sexual perspective?

The following questions relate to money and security. Again, men and women see this aspect of the relationship and their role in the world differently. The following questions are designed to explore value differences between you.

How important is having money in the bank to you?

Do you and your partner combined finances or keep them separate?

Do you have separate bank accounts or a joint account?

Is money more important to you or what you can do with it?

The Neuro-Com Program

Do you believe that you will always have sufficient money to do what you wish with it?

_____

Is money more important to you than being loved?

_____

Do you think money is important to your partner?

_____

Is financial security important to you at this point in time?

_____

What does financial security mean to you in terms of possessions, job, business, and so on?

_____

_____

_____

_____

Do you believe that you and your partner have sufficient money to live on a day-by-day basis?

_____

Do you save money to be used for holidays and other leisure activities with your partner?

_____

The following questions relate to the way you communicate with your partner. Often, individuals see the need to communicate differently, and this can create serious conflict.

Do you and your partner talk to each other openly and often?

_____

Which of you tends to talk the most?

_____

Are you comfortable talking about problems or issues that your partner may raise?

_____

Are you comfortable talking about things of little importance, or do you prefer to speak only of important issues?

_____

Do you have periods during which you do not talk to each other and if so what is the usual cause of these silences?

_____

Does your partner say things that annoy you?

_____

Give as many examples as you can about such annoying conversations or comments.

_____

_____

_____

_____

Do you like the way your partner speaks to you in tone and attitude?

What do you like about the way your partner communicates with you?

What do you dislike about the way your partner communicates with you?

Do you have interests in common (sports, world affairs, hobbies etc.)? If so, what are they?

Do you support your partner by engaging in or actively approving interests that you do not share?

Would you go out of your way or spend your own time supporting your partners interests even if you had no desire to do so?

I repeat my earlier warning about doing this exercise with an open mind about your view of your partner. Keep in mind that the simple fact that unless you or your partner are both willing to review your relationship values using the Neuro-Com strategies, neither of you will change anything. The common idea that one person can change another is a complete fallacy, unless that person understands the need to change, and is willing to do so.

So, don't expect that just doing this exercise will create change. In fact, you must be prepared for a deep discussion of your differences and to evaluate if your ability to accept these differences is strong enough. Without tolerating and accepting your partner's values, and thus their behaviours, relationships never work. If you view your relationship from a purely selfish perspective, your relationship is already doomed.

To further enhance your awareness of your wider values, make a list of the people, places, and events that you both value so that you can evaluate what is really important to you in a positive, happiness-producing awareness.

In relationships, knowing your partner, and your commonalities and differences is a very empowering place to be. If you both do these exercises, you will learn a great deal about each other. But, as I said earlier, you may be also left wondering why you are even with the person you are with!

As you move through this exercise you may notice that there seems to be something consistent in the things you value in each category. You may also notice that the things you value are similar between categories. The more time you spend on this exercise, the more you will realise that you are truly programmed with a set of values that have directed every part of your life: the people to whom you are attracted, the places you go, and the things you do.

So now you know where each of you stands and the values variations you each have, take a look at how you express these values in your behaviours if they create conflict. Look at how you see each other and how you feel about each other. Remember the three foundations of a great relationship: trust, respect and acceptance for the things you don't jointly value. Do you have these? What is missing?

Use your understanding of your personal Neuro-Com patterns to increase the energy in values that support and foster your relationship and to reduce the energy in values that are damaging or destructive to your relationship.

This exercise will allow you to see your partner in a different light with a greater degree of compassion, love and acceptance. Go all the way and you may well create a "soul" partnership.

CHAPTER NINE

Where to from Here?

NEURO-COM AND SPIRITUAL EVOLUTION

I want to briefly discuss the role of religion in our lives and how the traditional religions fit into our model of the mind. It is not appropriate to go into a lengthy treatise on religion, but it is important that you are comfortable with knowing how the programming affects you and how your understanding of consciousness fits into a higher model. I have no doubt that I will incur the wrath of many readers, but the need to discuss it comes from the fact that religions are major part of the distress the human race continues to create within groups, nations, and philosophies.

Only recently have large numbers of people started to reject religions. Although you may now reject religion, they still maintain a very strong hold of your belief and values system unless you are a Neuro-Com Master and have totally disconnected their influence. Religions have brought us many of our social values of right and wrong, and consequently inform our legal system.

Despite this, many who have rejected the formal religions still search for meaning that is greater than they are. From this desire, the New Age movement was born, with thousands of philosophies espousing their own version of truth.

I have studied religions and their role in human evolution for more than 40 years and have approached the subject as two separate studies:

- The core of all religious thought
- The dogma that man has buried the truth in

Most of what is taught is dogma. It is information that the power brokers of the religions have written about and preached because they found they could maintain their power through the use of guilt and fear. You may notice that the most powerful religions are also the wealthiest. They have controlled their flocks by teaching about an omnipotent God who would cast them into Hell if they misbehaved in any way that did not following the laws of the church. On the other hand, the blow is softened by teaching that this seemingly malicious God is also caring toward those who blindly follow and offer money and support for the church.

You have probably detected a little cynicism in my words. This is because 90% of my stress management clients came to me because of guilt and fear derived from illogical family and culturally held religious instruction.

I don't want to pursue this line in this book, but it is important to understand the core of religious thought. None of the great religious thinkers view their God as a structured image of an omnipotent being with a penchant for destruction or even for interfering with human existence. A close search of the Bible and its key players shows an interesting phenomenon.

God clearly refers to Himself by the name "I Am". Think about the connotations of this. "I Am" means that it exists NOW, in this moment. It doesn't say "I was" or "I will be." These are the realms of your unconscious mind. "I Am" is referring to NOW, and NOW is only accessed in consciousness.

All the great religions refer to a state known as enlightenment, nirvana, or grace. Millions of people around the world have put themselves through unbelievable rituals to try to achieve this elusive state. Few ever find it, and those that genuinely do usually avoid publicity. Being able to live in this moment, in NOW is perhaps the greatest gift you can give to yourself. By being CONSCIOUS, no longer reacting to your past emotional memory, and having no demands on your projected future means you are living in a state of absolute harmony. There is no conflict in this place.

Here there are no mood swings, no angers, fears, or guilt. Here you are on the "middle path" of the Tao, living the "enlightenment" of Buddha, in a state of grace of Christianity.

Would you like to achieve such a state?

The core of the representation of mind I have presented in this program is the core of this state. Consciousness is "Godhead." We are all part of this whole. Our unconscious memory is what separates us from that whole and makes us believe we are individuals. This understanding has nothing to do with religion, just an understandable connection between all of us as human beings.

We can also take this view a little further. When you look at our current understanding of matter, we know we are dealing with pure energy. Nothing exists in a form we know as solid. We also know that conscious thought can change our environment and create anything we wish to. It is only our restrictive beliefs about our capabilities that stop consciousness from doing it.

What if you learned to communicate with your unconscious mind in a way that deleted the emotional content from it? What if that process allowed you to stop the endless mind chatter and allowed you to live in NOW, in pure consciousness?

The strategies you have learned here give you the power to create such an outcome. What value do you place on this? In the words of Helen Mallicoat:

> I was regretting the past
> And fearing the future.
> Suddenly, my Lord was speaking.
> "My name is I Am."
>
> He paused. I waited. He continued.
>
> "When you live in the past,
> with its mistakes and regrets,
> it is hard. I am not there.
> My name is not "I Was."

> When you live in the future,
> with its problems and fears,
>
> It is hard. I am not there.
> My name is not "I Will Be."
>
> When you live in this moment,
> it is not hard. I am here.
> My name is "I Am!"

My path, as a result of my studies of the mind and deep exploration of hundreds of side tracks, has brought me to a very comfortable place, and I would like to share it with you. Over many decades, my mind as evolved into the principals of Cheyzen, a modern mind understanding of Zen based on Neuro-Com principals. If you have completed the exercises in this book, you will already know the incredible power of Neuro-Com to create change, remove anxiety and allow you to create your future.

This book is not the place to go into Cheyzen in depth. If you would like to continue your journey in this direction, please spend some time at www.cheyzen.org. If you like what you see, please contact me. I would be delighted to hear your thoughts. It is through like-minded people with an understanding of reality who can change the future of the human race. If you have made it this far on the journey, it is highly likely you are part of that future.

THE END AND THE BEGINNING

So now we come to the end of the program and the beginning of new life.

Please use your new power wisely to create a future for yourself and others around you. I would appreciate your feedback via our support website so I can continue to add useful strategies and tools that others may be able to use.

Good luck for all your future moments in NOW. May you live in peace and experience the wonders of the universe and all it has to offer.

CPSIA information can be obtained at www.ICGtesting.com
Printed in the USA
LVOW12s1659180514

386161LV00006B/5/P